Growing Up with Two Languages

A practical guide for the bilingual family

Third Edition

Una Cunningham

Routledge
Taylor & Francis Group

LONDON AND NEW YORK

First published 1999
by Routledge
Second edition published 2004
by Routledge
This edition published 2011
by Routledge
2 Park Square, Milton Park, Abingdon, Oxon, OX14 4RN

Simultaneously published in the USA and Canada
by Routledge
711 Third Avenue, New York, NY 10017

Routledge is an imprint of the Taylor & Francis Group, an informa business

British Library Cataloguing in Publication Data
A catalogue record for this book is available from the British Library

Library of Congress Cataloging in Publication Data
Cunningham-Andersson, Una, 1960-
    Growing up with two languages : a practical guide for the bilingual
family / Una Cunningham. – 3rd ed.
        p. cm.
    Includes bibliographical references and index.
    1. Bilingualism in children. 2. Parenting. I. Title.
    P115.2.C86 2011
    404'.2083 – dc22
                2010049756

ISBN: 978-0-415-59851-4 (hbk)
ISBN: 978-0-415-59852-1 (pbk)
ISBN: 978-0-203-81467-3 (ebk)

Typeset in Bembo
by Taylor & Francis Books

MIX
Paper from
responsible sources
FSC
www.fsc.org   FSC® C004839

Printed and bound in Great Britain by
TJ International Ltd, Padstow, Cornwall

Contents

Preface viii

Acknowledgements xi

1 Families with two languages 1

Background 1
Mixed language families and intercultural marriage 1
Minority language families 8

2 Expecting a child in a bilingual home 12

What do you want for your child? 12
Making plans 20
Be prepared! 25

3 The family language system 31

Developing a system 31
One person–one language 35
One language–one location (minority language at home) 44
'Artificial' bilingualism 47

4 Language development 51

Active and passive languages 54
Interference and mixing 57
The critical period hypothesis 62

5   **The child with two languages**   65

Advantages and disadvantages of two languages for the child   65
Being different   67
Day-care and school   71

6   **Practical parenting in a bilingual home**   78

Help your child to make the most of the situation   78
Home language education and Saturday schools   79
Practical advice for parents whose child has two languages   82
Things to do at home   85

7   **Competence in two cultures**   93

Access to two cultures   93
Religion   98
Achieving cultural competence   99

8   **Problems you may encounter**   110

Quality of input   110
Semilingualism   113
Changed circumstances   115
Children with special needs   121

9   **Keeping it up**   124

Motivation   124
Teenagers   126
Advice from other parents   130

10 **Looking back on a bilingual childhood**   135

Grown-up children   135
The next generation   135
Cases   136
Conclusion   164

11 **Research and further reading**   165

Advantages and possible disadvantages of bilingualism   166
How bilingual acquisition works   168
How bilingual speakers use their languages   172

Appendix A: Organising a workshop on raising children
           with two languages   174

Appendix B: Ways to support a child's development
           in two languages   177

Parent and children groups   177
Minority language play-school   178
Saturday school   180

Appendix C: Documenting a child's linguistic
           development   181

Vocabulary   181
Length of utterance   182
Language mixing   182
Pronunciation   183

Glossary   185
Bibliography   187
Index   191

Preface

For those, like me, who grew up using a single language except during foreign language lessons at school, it is a new experience to live great chunks of life through the medium of another language and culture. Even if the second language involved is one that was learned at school, its daily use involves new challenges and rewards. All sorts of issues must be addressed depending on the circumstances, such as the choice of language to be spoken to which people in which situation, and how those involved will acquire reasonable facility in their second language, and what relationship they will have to the non-native culture.

This book is intended for parents who find their everyday life involves two or more languages. The readers I have in mind are not generally part of an established bilingual community in a country, but rather individuals or families who have uprooted and resettled in another linguistic environment, or their partners or children. This raises fascinating issues, such as the question of what it is not to be a native speaker of a language, with full access to the associated culture, and how best to hold your own as a non-native. I will not try to tell you how best to learn a second language, but rather what the effects of dealing with two languages may be for you or your children. There are so many of us in the same boat. Let us learn from each other!

This book is the third edition of a book originally published in 1999, with the second edition in 2004. The first two editions were co-authored by my husband, Staffan Andersson. This time I am the sole author, but I can assure readers that our marriage and partnership continue! The parts of the text that refer to my own children have been updated, and the sections relating to older children and teenagers have been extended to reflect our experiences. Two new chapters have been added, one with interviews from adults and older teens looking back on a bilingual childhood and one with an overview of relevant research into the field of childhood bilingualism, with tips for further reading for students and other interested readers. The appendix dealing with Internet resources has been taken out, as this kind of information is much more useful on a website, and the book now has its own companion website, with links to useful and interesting resources and the possibility of interaction with and between readers. There are also sound files available from the website, with excerpts from some of the interviews in the new Chapter 10. In the years that have passed since the first edition was published the main thing that has changed is that our children have grown older. Leif is now 24, Anders is 22, Patrik is 18 and Lisa is 16. The long-term results of my family's own venture with two languages have turned out better than we dared to hope. Two of our four children, Anders and Lisa, are now native-like in both their languages and the other two are very competent in English, but native-like in Swedish only. This is partly a result of differences in their schooling, as both Lisa and Anders attended English-medium schools for periods, but it is, in my opinion, at least as much the result of individual differences in interest in and aptitude for language.

I am an immigrant to Sweden (I was brought up in Northern Ireland), a foreign language learner (having studied Irish, French and Spanish at school and Portuguese and Vietnamese later in life), a second language learner (I lived in Spain for a year while a student in 1979–80 and first came into contact with the Swedish language in 1980, at the age of 20) and a parent of four children who have grown up with two languages and cultures.

When my children were small, I often felt the need for some kind of manual to consult. Just as we have a family medical book and a child development book, we would like to have been able to look up the answers to our questions concerning life with two languages and cultures. There are excellent books which help parents and teachers deal with children with two languages, such as those by George Saunders (1982), Lenore Arnberg (1987) and Colin Baker (1995), and a number of books dealing with the way bilingual children learn their languages have been written since the first edition of this book appeared. The main difference between this book and others is the number of families whose experiences are tapped here, particularly in this third edition, with the addition of material from some 20 new interviews.

For anyone who is curious about my story, Staffan and I met as backpackers on 16 July 1980 on a train in Nis, in what was then Yugoslavia, when Staffan was travelling from Uppsala to the Black Sea and I from Nottingham to Israel. Neither of us reached our destinations! We were married in 1985 and have now celebrated our silver wedding anniversary.

If you would like to contribute your own experiences for possible inclusion in a future edition of this book, or comment on any part of this book, please do not hesitate to get in touch with me through the book's webpages.

Good luck!

Acknowledgements

This book has benefited from input from personal accounts of life with two languages supplied by almost 200 individuals and families in the Internet community and in real life. They have generously shared their experiences of what has worked well or not so well when living with two languages within the family. We can learn a lot from the experiences of others who have faced the same issues as we do now and have had to deal with them. Thank you all of you who have given us a glimpse of your lives with two or more languages!

For Leif, Anders, Patrik and Lisa, who taught us what we know about children.

Chapter 1

Families with two languages

Background

There have always been those who have moved from one country to another to study or work for a while. The expansion of the European Union (EU) has led to ever-increasing numbers of Europeans who move from one country to another within Europe. In addition, many people have come to the countries of Western Europe as refugees from conflicts in other parts of the world or in what was once Yugoslavia. In Japan, Korea and Taiwan, as well as parts of the Middle East, Africa and South America, there are many foreign workers, often married to local people. The USA, Canada and Australia have, by their very nature, large immigrant populations. People are living abroad all over the world for innumerable reasons.

The reasons behind a move from one country to another have a lot to do with how the move will turn out. If a family goes to live in another country because one or both of the parents have got a job there, the situation is quite different from when a single person moves from one country to another to settle down with a native of the new country. Both these situations are radically different from that faced by refugee families who flee from a war zone to take refuge in a peaceful country. All of these immigrants have some things in common. They are all faced with learning the language and becoming familiar with the culture of their new country, but they probably have very contrasting expectations of how well they will succeed at these tasks and how long they are likely to stay in the new country. They are, therefore, not equally motivated to throw themselves into their new situations.

Mixed language families and intercultural marriage

Some adults who become involved with two languages are in the position that they have met and decided to live with a person who has a different first language from themselves. Two languages generally mean two cultures, although a couple can have separate cultures without speaking different languages. Examples of this are an American–British couple or a Mozambican–Portuguese couple, or even a couple where one comes from, say, northern Italy and the other from Sicily. This kind of relationship is fraught with potential misunderstandings and unspoken expectations and assumptions which need to be made explicit given the couple's lack of a common background. The more subtle the differences between the cultures involved, the less prepared they will be for these misunderstandings.

If each person in a couple speaks a different language and this is not the majority language of the place where they live they will need to give more thought to the way they want their languages to be used when they have a child.

Language choice

A family with two languages will usually find a regular way of defining how the languages are used, depending on where they live and how well each of the parents speaks the other's language. A French–German couple living in Germany may thus speak French between themselves and German in the company of others. If, however, they started out using one or other language together, perhaps because one of them did not then speak the other's language, they may not be able to change easily if there comes a time when it would make more sense to speak the other language. When children come along, they will need to be accommodated in the couple's linguistic arrangements.

Example

An American woman and a Swedish man met while they were both study-ing in Germany. They began by speaking German together. When they subsequently married and moved to Sweden they gradually started to speak English together. When the woman started learning Swedish she wanted them to speak Swedish together, which they still do, although it is alter-nated with English depending on the subject matter. When their son was born, they each spoke their own native language with him.

My own story is that I (from Northern Ireland) met Staffan (from Sweden) travelling in Eastern Europe. We had no choice but to speak English, our only common language. Later, when I moved to Sweden and learned Swedish, we continued to speak English together, because of our mutual reluctance to speak Swedish to each other, even when my knowledge of Swedish became greater than Staffan's knowledge of English. We each speak our own language with our children.

However the mixed language couple decide to organise their linguistic system, one or both of them will at any given time be using a language other than their own to communicate. The partner will be left with the task of talking and listening to a person who probably does not have full mastery of the language being used. The couple will, of course, become very used to this set-up, and no longer really hear any foreign accent or faulty grammar that the other may have. Their children, however, may delight in correcting their parents' non-native errors in each language, if they do not find them embarrassing.

To a certain extent, the non-native speaker will learn from the native speaker, but for most couples linguistic correctness cannot be allowed to stand in the way of communication. Not many people want to think about the correct form to be used when they are planning what to buy for supper; still less do they want to be corrected by their partner. The learning that does go on will most likely be on the level of absorbing the correct forms used by the native speaker. However, if the non-native speaker is not motivated to improve his or her language, finding it adequate for its purpose, it will probably remain at the same level, give or take a few new items of vocabulary. This is known as fossilisation.

Understanding each other

In some cases one parent may be totally uninterested in learning the other parent's language. Before the couple have children, this may never be a problem – both speak either the majority language or another common language. If the minority language parent wants to introduce his or her own language for the first time when speaking to the baby, the other parent may quickly begin to feel left out. This may provide the necessary motivation to learn the language in question, or it may become a major source of friction in the family, and might even thwart the whole idea of exposing the child to both parents' languages.

For parents who want to be able to speak their own language to their child, this can be very frustrating. If the other parent does not support the use of the minority language it will be almost impossible to make it an active part of family life. Children will quickly detect any signs of disapproval from a parent. Some families find that the baby and the majority language parent learn the minority language together, but the child's vocabulary will generally accelerate away from the parent's by the age of two. This can be minimised if the parent makes an active effort to learn the minority language.

Another option, which may in some cases be the only way to ensure that the child gets some input in the minority language, is to arrange a system whereby the minority language-speaking parent speaks that language with the child in all situations except when the other parent is present.

> I'd recommend anyone in an international marriage should do their best to master their spouse's language or their host country's language, not only for the sake of their marriage, but also for the children's sake. We can't demand from our children anything which we parents cannot accomplish. So our children will be bilingual and bicultural to the extent that we ourselves are.
>
> (John Moore, Japan)

> Michael has always corrected all my mistakes (grammar and pronunciation), making me repeat the same words over and over again until I could pronounce them correctly. This has been very helpful, and it still is.
>
> (Stephanie Lysee, USA)

> Both my husband and I are language teachers – but we have found that it is best not to teach each other. Kenjiro will sometimes correct me – but I think he takes care not to do it automatically, but to consider the time, place, occasion, and most of all my mood – it can be irritating to be corrected when what is really important is making sure that the garbage gets taken out, for instance.
>
> (Robin Nagano, Japan)

Language mixing

Most people who live for many years away from countries where their native language is spoken as the majority language find that their native language is affected in one way or another. The most obvious consequence is that it is difficult to remember words in your native language. You may find that words of your second language pop up when you are speaking or writing in your native language. If you associate with other speakers of your native language who like yourself have lived for years with the second language, you may find yourselves throwing in words of the majority language when they seem particularly apt or just because they come to mind first. This is in addition to the times when you need to use a majority language word to refer to something which exists only in the country you live in. Since there is no risk of not being understood, this language mixing can sometimes be a real characteristic of this kind of speech:

> I find myself searching for words, and am most comfortable speaking with other long-term residents who also speak Japanese and then we can mix in phrases without having to worry about it.
>
> (Robin Nagano, Japan)

A family with two languages may in time develop their own hotch-potch of the two languages. The reasons for this are varied, but one reason is that parents might find it simpler to avoid minority language words that they know the child will not understand, using the majority language instead. Of course, if parents mix their languages in this way in the children's hearing, they should not be surprised if the children learn to do so too!

MOTHER: 'Let's go and pick some blåbar' (compare with 'Kom ska vi plocka blåbar' and 'Let's go and pick some bilberries').

LEIF (4;0): 'Först ska jag climba upp, sen ska jag slida ner' (compare with 'First I'll climb up, then I'll slide down' and 'Forst ska jag klattra upp, sen ska jag åka ner').

This is slightly different from the kind of mixing where the nouns and verbs of one language may be borrowed into the other language and given that language's endings. This kind of borrowing of English words into Swedish is a common feature of language used in comput-ing and the like, where people 'mejlar' (*skickar*, send) email to each other and look at 'sajter' (*webbplatser*, sites) on the Internet.

My children have found that from about the age of 10–12 their monolingual Swedish friends were likely to tease them about any mixing in of Swedish words in their English. What happens is that the Swedish youngsters are listening closely to the English spoken and trying to follow it as best they can. They are then really surprised to hear the odd Swedish word. This has given rise to a system whereby English is set as the only permissible language in, for example, the car on a ride to town for the so-called monolingual Swedish children as well as for those who have grown up with both languages. This game is thoroughly enjoyed by all. Obviously, this technique will not be helpful in all combinations of minority languages and countries of residence, but it worked for us in Sweden, where Swedish 12-year-olds can speak English well enough for informal conversation.

Now that they are older they are able to reflect on the kind of mixing and switching they use:

> I can easily switch between languages in a way I know other people can't. It's no big deal for me to incorporate foreign words into my conversations. It happens quite a lot. I use English words in my everyday language, which is quite common for people my age, but perhaps I use it a bit more. And it happens that I use other languages, German words, which is not a big thing for me but other people notice, oh you used German now. I think I use the same English words in Swedish as other people but more, and I think I use more expressions than other Swedish kids. I can sometimes say a whole sentence in English where other people won't. Also, when I think about it I sometimes use expressions in Swedish which have English grammar or which are English idioms.
>
> (Patrik, 18;0)

> It depends who I'm talking to. Some people I keep it very clean which language is which language, while some people I speak Swedish to I will switch maybe even several times in a sentence. These are people who are very proficient in both Swedish and English. And so it makes more sense to be as precise as possible, switching and then switching in a language. It often happens sub-consciously. People will tell me that wasn't a very sensible sentence in any language, but it makes sense put together. Sometimes it is conscious. I definitely don't do it if I'm speaking to someone I know doesn't really speak English. Then it doesn't make any sense; they wouldn't understand me. I have to think more about it so I can express it.
>
> (Anders, 21;9)

Language switching

An additional problem in the mixed language family may arise if any of them are in the habit of speaking the minority language in public: the family may be perceived as tourists in their own country. Even minority language speakers are probably quite fluent in the language of the country in which they live, and problems may arise if the minority language is reasonably well known as a school language, for example English or German in Sweden. The family risk being addressed in the minority language by well-meaning shop assistants. This puts them in the awkward situation of having to decide whether to answer in the majority language, embarrassing the shop assistants, who may feel that they have been eavesdropping, or carrying on the conversation in the minority language without revealing that they are also proficient in the majority language.

Example

My husband and I generally speak English together, even in public. On one occasion we went into a bookshop in Uppsala, still talking together. We approached the counter and I asked in good Swedish for a particular (English) title. We then followed the assistant to the shelf, where he turned to Staffan and said in English, 'I think this is the one you are looking for'. To say anything other than 'Thank you' would have been churlish. The assistant had obviously assumed that I was speaking English with Staffan because he knew no Swedish.

One problem that I have is that I don't like to speak English outside the home. When I speak English to my children, people assume that I don't know Hebrew (even though my children often answer in Hebrew) and they try to speak to me in English. I find this very aggravating, as my Hebrew is excellent and I don't want to sound or feel like an 'outsider'.

(Bari Nirenberg, Israel)

Communication

Depending on the level of mastery that the non-native speaker has in the language spoken by the parents, communication may be more or less affected by the presence of two languages. Native speakers may find that they need to use relatively simple language when talking to their partner. There may be misunderstandings even when they both believe the non-native speaker has understood. A question like 'Do you know what I mean?' can be answered in the affirmative by someone who knows what they think you mean, without the misunderstanding ever becoming clear.

Of course, even using simple language becomes a habit, and does not really have to limit the level of conversation. It is possible to talk in simple terms about even the most complex matters if both parties are sufficiently interested. If parents usually talk to each other in the minority language, majority language speakers will most likely become very fluent in this language, in the sense of being able to speak at normal speed and without hesitation, even if their speech is accented and full of grammatical errors. This facilitates the couple's communication, making it less arduous for both parties. This is not really very different from the kind of practised communication any couple develop after many years together.

Minority language families

Minority language families have two adults who are both speakers of the same language, but it is not the majority language in the society in which they live. In some ways, they are in a much easier situation than the mixed language couple. Whether they originally met in their home country or in the country where they now live (or elsewhere), they have a lot in common. They form together an island of the minority language and culture in an ocean of foreignness. They can face the new culture and language in which they find themselves, and sometimes close the door on it and retire inside to a home life full of familiarity. The situation can vary depending upon the family's circumstances and the reason for their move.

Children in these families can make a clear distinction between the home and the world outside. A family who move as a unit from one country to another to work bring a whole way of life with them. They expect to go on much as they did at home. There can be many reasons why such a family relocate. If it is for a limited time, they probably plan to go back to their country of origin after a number of years as temporary residents. These people are often well educated and work in universities or in multinational companies or organisations, such as the many American and British people working in Swedish universities or the international scene in the institutions and organisations of Brussels or Strasbourg. They may prefer to remain apart from the local community as far as possible, and place their children in international schools. They might not bother much with learning the local language unless it is necessary for their work, and may associate almost exclusively with others of their kind. They see themselves as ex-pats and keep closely in touch with what is going on at home, via newspapers, radio and satellite television. It is clear to them that they are living abroad, and they have no aspiration to become part of the society in which they are temporarily living.

Immigrants and refugees

There are many thousands of refugees in Europe, who have come from conflicts and disasters in many countries. They often intend to return to their own countries when the situation there improves, but may live in exile longer than they originally planned. Refugee families often have the same kind of outlook on their stay in the new country as those who are in a country temporarily for work purposes. They may plan to return to their own country as soon as conditions improve, and so are not really interested in getting too involved with their new country. They have brought their language and culture with them. They may not feel motivated to learn the new language, and may find that their children are soon much better able to communicate with people in the new country than they are. The adults in such families often have extreme difficulty in getting any kind of employment in their new country, and if they do manage to get a job it is unlikely to correspond to their qualifications and capacity. These families often associate primarily with others like themselves and keep themselves informed about the situation in their homeland. Unfortunately, things do not always turn out according to plan. After a period of time has passed, it may become clear that the refugee family are unlikely to return home in the foreseeable future. Perhaps the political situation in their country of origin is not improving, or perhaps their children have become so firmly rooted in the soil of the host country that a move back home would be disastrous. At this point the family need to take a fresh look at their situation in the new country, and maybe take steps to improve their skills in the language and look at their employment prospects. However, the very fact that there is an intact language and culture in the home is likely to ensure that the parents in the family will not become fully integrated into the society of the new country. The situation for their children is, of course, different. They will usually learn to master the language and culture fairly quickly, and may prefer and expect to live in the new country always.

This is the position for many refugees from Chile and other parts of Latin America living in Sweden. They did not expect to stay long in Sweden and settled down to live together, so that they rarely had any need to speak any language other than Spanish. Time went by, however, without any prospect of being able to return. The refugees' children attended Swedish schools and became fluent in Swedish, often acting as interpreters for their parents when they needed to communicate in Swedish with the authorities or doctors. Eventually, it became impossible to leave Sweden where the children had settled down. To then start learning Swedish after a number of years was impossible for many – it would have been like saying that they would never return to their home countries. In some countries, for example Germany and Sweden, there are thousands of immigrant workers who were brought in from Turkey and Greece and other countries during the 1960s and 1970s when there was work for everyone and jobs waiting for any ambitious person wanting to come and make their fortune. Many of these workers returned to their countries of origin, but quite a few settled permanently in their new countries. This kind of immigration has basically stopped in many countries.

Citizens of the EU are allowed to work in any of the other EU countries, and unemployed people may go to look for work elsewhere in the EU for three months without losing their unemployment benefit from home. Many do find work, despite a generally high level of unemployment in Europe. Others start their own businesses, and manage to make a living that way in a new country.

International employees

If, as is often the case, the family come to the new country because one of the parents has got a job there, the other parent may or may not be allowed to work. Even if allowed to do so, the latter is unlikely to find a paying job on the open market, given a persistent generally high level of unemployment. Some companies may have a scheme whereby accompanying spouses are able to work part time for the company, but this is not usually the case. This means that the working parent may easily be able to meet people and interact socially, while the other is left at home, often with children. Some international companies which recruit personnel from abroad take great pains to help accompanying families find their feet; others do nothing. Ideally the company should offer support at all stages, with locally employed staff specifically recruited to smooth the integration of newcomers from abroad.

Schools and pre-schools need to be investigated. International schools may be available, where teaching is in the medium of English or other languages, which might be better for the children if the stay is not expected to be longer than a couple of years. Otherwise they may do better to learn the local language. This depends on the children's age and inclination. Some countries have systems whereby children can do their schoolwork by correspondence from the home country. Modern online education solutions will probably do their bit to make this option better and more popular in the future. It may be possible for children to attend a local school part time, say four mornings a week, and concentrate on the work sent from the home-country school the rest of the time. This way they get the best of both worlds. The company should make information about this kind of arrangement available to their international employees.

Part of the fun in living abroad is the attraction of getting to know a new culture, and maybe learning a new language. Even though many international companies have English as their working language, knowledge of the local language can certainly make the stay more meaningful, particularly for the accompanying family members. It would be very helpful for newcomers if the company held classes in the local language and culture.

Visiting academics

International companies may be reasonably motivated to look after their employees' welfare and ensure that the accompanying family adapts as well as possible. The situation can be a lot worse in other organisations, for example academic institutions. Typically universities make little or no effort to help their international undergraduates and postgraduates find their feet. They do even less for their families. In the case of visiting lecturers or professors they may help out with the task of finding accommodation, but this is usually done at the departmental level rather than through any central organisation.

The success of a period abroad depends to a great extent on how well the accompanying family adapt to their new surroundings. For the one who actually has the job, there is often not a problem, but the difficulty in getting to know people in a new country can be frustrating for an accompanying husband or wife who is trying to make the best of their new role as home-maker in a strange place. Of course, this is easier in some places than in others. But even in countries where people are chatty and open, it would be naive to believe that you are likely to slip into the local people's social life after a couple of months.

Many families in this position tend to centre their social life around others with the same linguistic and cultural background. Even those who have lived many years in the same country often find that they associate almost exclusively in their free time with other foreigners, even if they are not from the same country. The very fact that they are foreigners together is enough to give them something in common.

Chapter 2

Expecting a child in a bilingual home

Any couple's first child is awaited with a certain amount of trepidation. Nobody can be sure whether they will actually like parenthood or be able to do what is required until they have become parents. For the couple who live with two languages, for whatever reason, there are many additional questions. They must think through their linguistic situation and make a place in it for the child, just as they might prepare a corner of their bedroom for the baby's cradle.

What do you want for your child?

This is the most important question the prospective parents must ask themselves. Depending on the parents' circumstances and their plans for the future, they will regard different things as important. A couple who plan to stay only a few years in a country before returning to their mutual home country will want to plan differently from a family where one parent has immigrated permanently to the other's country, or parents who want their child to speak a language which neither of them speaks natively, where a second language is introduced artificially. Some of the following considerations may be relevant.

Speaking an immigrant parent's language

Even if you have married a foreigner and moved to his or her country to make your life together, you probably want to ensure that your child learns your language, and not just the majority language which almost everybody around you speaks. It is enough to live with a speaker of another language: you may not want to raise one! Of course, your child will learn the majority language, but it need not be from you, at least not in the early stages. Many parents living outside a country where their own language is spoken feel that being able to speak their own language to their children is a vital part of their relationship. No matter how well you know the majority language, it can be difficult to talk to a tiny baby in that language, to sing and play and scold and comfort without the resources learned in your own childhood.

However, if the parents decide for whatever reason that one or both of them should speak to the child in a language other than their own, it can be done, although there may be a price to pay in the relationship between parent and child in later years. A mother faced with a rebellious teenager may be better equipped to counter defiance and rhetoric in her own language, and will perhaps command more respect and credibility in the child's eyes than if she is a less than perfect speaker of the majority language, which the child probably masters totally.

Some mixed language families arrange for the minority language to be spoken by both parents to the child, at least at home. This solution means that one parent speaks a non-native language to the child, at least some of the time, and may feel awkward. The relationship between parents and children is so special that it is a shame to introduce what some may perceive as a barrier – a non-native language. However, this solution gives the minority language a head start, which will let the child become more competent in that language in the early years. Some parents are concerned that their children may be at a disadvantage if they do not speak or understand the majority language very well before starting kindergarten or pre-school, but experience shows that children are exceptional language learners and usually catch up. The warnings that have been raised have generally concerned children from communities where there is little opportunity to hear native speakers of the majority language.

In cases where one parent is equally at home with both languages, other options are open, for example that parent can speak either language with the child, depending on who else is present. Parents who have themselves grown up with two languages may well feel they want to interact with their child in both their languages.

Belonging to a minority group in the country of residence

If the family's minority language is spoken by many people in the same area, so that it is meaningful to talk about an immigrant or ex-pat community, it may be important that the child is able to become part of that community. The family's social life may be spent largely within such a group, so that the child needs to know enough of the minority language to be able to participate in various activities, such as going to religious services, play-group and maybe Saturday school or even ordinary school, through the medium of that language:

> Like many immigrants, we socialised in the well-established Armenian ethnic community in New York. I attended Saturday Armenian school and therefore was literate as well.
>
> (Suzanne Hovanesian, USA)

Other examples of this kind of minority community are the Finnish community in Sweden, the Greek-Cypriot community in London or the English community in Brussels. Members of these communities tend to have a lot of contact with each other and many activities are aimed at passing on the minority language and culture to the children.

Feeling at home in the immigrant parent's home country

Many people who have emigrated will want to return regularly to their home country to visit friends and relatives and to keep a lingering homesickness at bay. Sometimes immigrants may hunger for the feeling of being as fully linguistically and culturally competent as they were before they left their native country. The feeling can in part be recreated by a visit to that country, although both the country and the individual will have changed in the intervening years. Immigrants may wish their children to feel at home in the country that they themselves once left. They may even wish their children to live in that country in the future, or at least to study there or choose a marriage partner from there. This can be a major reason for some parents ensuring that their children become proficient in the minority language:

> I would raise my children speaking Spanish, so they don't lose their cultural background. It kills me to see Hispanic children not knowing their native tongue. Now I know how my parents felt.
>
> (Marc Rod, Florida)

> They never can tell when they will meet people of their culture. They need to know that this is their origin. They need to incorporate themselves into society, even if they don't live in Nigeria. Wherever they live they need to be able to speak my language and embrace that culture. They are not English.
>
> (Grace, from Nigeria, living in Sweden)

I am very much aware of how much of my culture they do not share. They know the geography and social life of Ireland from their summers there. They know Irish music from recordings and from the fact that I have a number of musician friends, some of whom are very well known. They associate Irish music with me (once when I was away in China, they asked their mother to put a recording of Irish music on because they missed me).

(Sean Golden, Barcelona)

Being able to communicate with relatives

If an immigrant parent still has family members in the country of origin, it is important that the child can communicate with these people. Not only is it tragic if grandparents cannot speak to their grandchildren, but also it can be important for the child to realise that the immigrant parent has a background and a family:

I spoke less and less German once I entered school and did not speak any at all, except isolated words or greetings, from about age eight till 14. That spring my German grandparents visited and I was very ashamed at not being able to speak with them.

(William C. Brown, Delaware)

There came a moment when they were about four to five years old when they rebelled and complained bitterly about my addressing them in English. I was the only father who did so, it made them feel 'different'. They said no one else around us spoke English. Fortunately, this happened in June, just before we went to Ireland, where they would be together with their grandparents and aunts and uncles, and I could remind them that, in Ireland, nobody around them spoke Spanish, and that their grandparents wouldn't understand them if they spoke in Spanish.

(Sean Golden, Barcelona)

My eldest daughter did an exchange term in Copenhagen, where she actually found she understood everything. My relatives who met her said she also spoke Danish. My middle son always tries to speak Danish to my mother now that he is grown up. My youngest son understands and says a few sentences just for fun, but I think he keeps to Swedish. But they all love to go to Denmark, so every summer they want to come along with us. Now that they are grown up they seem to be a bit proud of having that contact as well.

> (Pia, herself brought up with Danish parents in Sweden, of her children, who were raised in Swedish)

My relatives were very thrilled! They knew my mother did not speak Turkish to me, so they supported my effort. It was not just a matter of language, but also wanting to know what being Turkish was, and wanting to know myself. They considered it as a compliment, so it was well received.

> (Benjamin, raised in Swedish in Sweden, now living in Istanbul)

In the case of a mixed marriage where one partner is from the country of residence, the children's picture of their parents' childhood can be very unbalanced. The children might meet their grandparents, uncles, aunts and cousins on, say, the father's side very often, perhaps even daily. They might even live in the same house as their father grew up in, go to the same school as their father did, play in the same places and swim at the same beaches. The father will be able to share his childhood with his children in a very concrete way. If the mother gets no opportunity to share her upbringing with her children, they may get the impression that she has no background; that she just appeared fully grown out of the earth, without the substance of family behind her. It can be very important for the mother in such a situation that the children have the linguistic and cultural competence to be able to form real relationships with members of her family, and to be able to participate fully in whatever is happening on visits to her home country:

> We spent whole summers in Italy. But I can remember very clearly when I was much younger, about six or seven, I couldn't really communicate in Italian with my Italian relations. I don't know why, maybe I was just used to my mother's Italian – English Italian.
>
> (Loretta, brought up with Italian and English in England)

> In the holidays, from June to August we went to the northern area and they were all speaking Hindko there so I understood what they were saying and they understood me in Pashto and Hindko. It was no problem.
>
> (Nazir, raised with Hindko, Pashto, Urdu and Punjabi in Pakistan)

Absolute balanced bilingualism or getting by?

Some couples, especially those who do not have much contact with other bilingual families, talk of bringing up their children to be bilingual, by which they may mean to be equally competent in two languages, and to be indistinguishable from monolingual native speakers in both languages. This is, in our opinion, an unrealistic ambition in many cases, if the family does not spend almost equal amounts of time in countries where the languages are spoken. Balanced bilingualism means that both languages are equally strong. This is often difficult to achieve while the children are small, but may not be unachievable in the long term in some cases, given sufficient motivation on the part of the children themselves. Many parents in mixed and minority language families report that their children's dominance in the languages involved goes in waves. The minority language may be stronger while they are small, while the other takes over when they start school. The minority language may be temporarily stronger during extended trips to a country where it is spoken, only to be put back into place on the return home.

Children growing up with the majority language as dominant may become more balanced if they later spend a term or a year at school in a country where the minority language is spoken. There are many exchange schemes, both within Europe and elsewhere, which arrange for youngsters to spend a period abroad, living in a family in the host country. These schemes may require the exchange student's family to act as hosts for a young person from another country for an equivalent period of time. A young person who has grown up with the language of the host country as a second language has a chance to develop full competence in the language at this stage. This opportunity is not usually available to those who learned the language only as a foreign language at school. Only the most exceptionally talented among such students will be able to speak the language of the host country without a foreign accent. There is reason to believe that young people who have been exposed to two languages from a very young age can learn to speak both languages without a foreign accent:

> Sometimes I make a big effort to sound native. If I don't get too many questions I can pull it off.
> (Benjamin, raised in Swedish in Sweden with
> passive exposure to Turkish, now living
> in Istanbul)

But after I finished school, actually I spent part of my gap year in Iran, and when I came back I made a conscious effort to speak more Farsi with my mum.

(Adam, raised with Czech and Farsi in Scotland)

Parents who expected their children to be indistinguishable from monolingual native speakers may be disappointed to hear their child speak the minority language with a foreign accent, or with obvious interference from the majority language. Languages in contact generally influence each other, and the problem may become less in time if the child receives sufficient input in both languages. Time spent in an environment where only the minority language is heard is very valuable:

His Canadian cousins think that he has an accent, and he doesn't like that at all. He wants to have a Canadian accent. ... But I don't think a stranger in Vancouver would pick him out as Swedish. They might pick him out as from a different part of the country or from the United States – not local.

(Claire, from Canada, in Sweden)

Even worse is if the children have interference the other way, from the minority language to the majority language, especially if the majority language is their dominant language (as it usually is for school-age children, unless they are being schooled in the minority language). It is important for everybody to fully master one language, regardless of how many other languages they know. Children who are experiencing difficulty in their dominant language need help to work on the problem areas, be they vocabulary, syntax or pronunciation. It may be necessary to get expert help from a speech therapist, or other person, if one can be found with experience of bilingual families, but parents can themselves help their children if they are aware that there is a problem. Suggestions for supporting a child's linguistic development will be found in Appendix B.

I'd say I am native in some parts in both languages and some parts only in one language. I can't say I am completely native in either language.

(Anders, 21;9)

His teacher complained that he had Swedish as a second language, which was a major uproar at our school. All the families who have their children in the bilingual programme should be bilingual families and they should have English before they start, and Swedish, and to have both languages as first languages, so halfway through elementary education to hear that your child is classified as having Swedish as a second language was really traumatic for all of us and we fought it tooth and nail, and we didn't think that the teacher who was deciding these issues was competent to decide the question. We actually went to a speech therapist about the issue. She was a specialist in bilingual children. She said that the criteria that the school was using were completely false. I think what happened was that his Swedish teacher at school wanted to have a certain level and he wasn't quite there. He occasionally mixed Swedish and English at school and she didn't want any mixing whatsoever. None whatsoever. Very strict. And so the speech therapist said that mixing is a natural way for bilingual children to learn. It comes as a question when the child speaks an English sentence and puts in a Swedish word it has the status of a question mark: what's the English word? I don't know what it is. And if you supply it, they immediately file that information.

(Anonymous, Sweden)

An advantage for adult life

Some parents see their children's prospective bilingualism as an asset for the future, almost as a qualification which will be useful to the children in their careers. This is particularly so if the language the children stand to learn has high status in the country in which the family live. There is more currency in the notion of English, Spanish or French being valuable for the children in their future careers than there is for languages such as Swedish, Catalan or Latvian, although, since nobody can tell what the future has in store for us or our children, you never know! Having access to a second language might be enough to build a career on, particularly if the language is less well known and not usually studied by speakers of the other language. In such a case, the young person with an excellent command of two languages may be in a strong position.

In an effort to give the child an advantageous start in life some parents take steps to expose their child to a second language which is not a native language for either of them. This can be done by placing the child in an international school or an immersion language programme, where the language of instruction is new to the child, by employing a foreign au pair to be with the children, or by having one or both of the parents speak a language which is not their native language with the child, either only at home or in all situations. In many parts of the world, children are introduced to a new language as the school language when they start school:

> In school, English, everything was in English.
>
> (Anthony, from Sierra Leone)

> After the age of four or five I went to school and in school it was our national language, which is Urdu. It was compulsory to speak only Urdu in the school, eight or nine hours a day.
>
> (Nazir, from Pakistan)

> At the time when I finished my primary school my mum discovered that, okay, she needs to go to a better school. Otherwise it's going to be tough. So she sent me to a military school, it was Command Secondary school, Lagos. The first time I went there it was pretty difficult for me, because I didn't know how to speak English. It was a problem for me. I was really at a disadvantage, I would say. People around me were speaking English.
>
> (Grace, from Nigeria)

> I started school when I was five and I remember the teacher would speak Spanish at that stage, the teacher I had, but later on it's been Catalan. So Catalan would be the language we would use normally, not just in Catalan, the subject, but in all the other subjects. Even English was taught in Catalan.
>
> (Pilar, from Catalonia)

Making plans

Before the birth of their first child, the couple who want to bring their child up with two languages or who themselves have two languages should think about and discuss the way they envisage their child's linguistic development. They need to think about who is going to speak which language to the child, and whether this will change according to the situation: whether they are at home or not, which country they are in, whether there are monolingual guests present, and so on. All this should be decided before the child is born because for many people it is extremely difficult to change the language you speak to a person once you have established a relationship in one language.

It may be helpful to meet and discuss this with others who are in a similar linguistic situation, especially if they have older children. Much can be learned just by spending time in such a family. Ask them how they arrange their use of the two languages, what rules or habits they have for who speaks what to whom in which situation, what problems they have encountered and how they have dealt with them. Look at how their children speak and understand the two languages. Later on at home you may want to discuss whether what you saw was the way you want things to turn out for your child. Learn from what the others did right, or if you want things to turn out differently try to find a way to make that happen for your child, given what you learned from the other family.

Try to get others to share their experiences with you. You may find that there are groups of families nearby who are raising children in the same or similar circumstances to you. You will find there are many channels to reach others on the Internet. You can get in touch with other parents and ask questions, and maybe even share your experiences with someone else (see the companion website).

After you have decided together how you want to arrange your child's exposure to the two languages, it might be a good idea to talk to both sets of grandparents about your plans. Grandparents are frequently conservative, and may be against the whole idea of bringing up the child with two languages. They may advise you to let the child concentrate on one language at a time or to completely forget the idea of 'confusing' the child with the minority language at all. This kind of advice is more likely to come from majority language grandparents who feel that they will be able to communicate with the child whatever happens.

Families who are temporarily abroad may be advised to try to return to their home country before their child starts school or pre-school to 'spare' the child the trouble of ever having to learn more than a smattering of the majority language. Another way of looking at this is that if you can plan a period abroad while your children are young you will be giving them an opportunity to be exposed to another language. You may be better able before the birth to explain the reasoning behind your decision to bring up your children with two languages in just the way you have planned. You may find that all kinds of people will want to offer advice. Health care experts also offer advice at times, although they might not be well informed about bilingualism. There are notable exceptions here, and at least in Sweden the public child health centres give out excellent brochures on raising children with two or more languages (see the companion website).

We had difficulties with the day-care centre when the oldest attended, and they kept trying to persuade me not to speak English as this was 'bad for her development'. But both my husband and I ignored them and tried to convince them of the value of two languages from the start.

(Nancy Holm, Sweden)

When my brother started school [he's older], a teacher told my parents not to worry about him being able to pick up English; that my parents should speak to him in our native language [Taiwanese] at home, and that the English would come at school. So, my parents speak both Taiwanese and English to us and I am *very* grateful. I can communicate with my relatives without an interpreter and can independently traverse throughout Taiwan.

(Linda Lee, USA)

Unfortunately, when we returned to the States, some jerk of a child psychologist told us to cease using French in her presence since it might disturb her little psyche. She has been in France and other Francophonic environments since, but still hesitates to use French in our presence. Like when she was a pre-schooler: 'Vas au lit.' 'I don't want to go to bed.'

(Merton Bland, USA)

Family life with two languages is easier than it looks. For those outside the situation of the bilingual family looking in, the complex of rules and conventions regulating who in the family speaks which language to other family members and the way these patterns change in the company of others looks daunting. But those involved are very used to the situation. For the children, language switching is as natural as breathing. After all, even in monolingual relationships every pair of people uses a different 'language': you do not speak in the same way to your husband as to your son, nor to your doctor as to your mother. The only difference in the bilingual set-up is that the various relationships require more than one language to be used.

A couple of weeks before the birth of our first child we happened to sit next to a mixed language family in a cafe. Of course, we had to eavesdrop. After quite a long while we managed to work out the rules. The father was an English speaker, and everybody except the mother spoke English to him and he answered in English. The mother was a Swedish speaker, and the children spoke Swedish to her and were answered in Swedish. The parents spoke Swedish together. When you know how it works, the conversation of a mixed language family is perfectly logical, but for outsiders listening to it the arrangement looks confusing and chaotic. The constant switching of languages according to who is speaking to whom might seem less orderly than it usually is:

> I spoke Swedish to my father and brothers and sister and English to my mother. It worked out well and it still works well. It's got a good flow to it and there's no problem for me. But it does confuse outsiders who come in and see it. The system has been established over many years and I can see how it is a bit confusing at first. But if you just understand the basic concept it's very simple.
>
> (Anders, 21;9)

What is in a name?

In the context of the mixed language couple, names take on a new significance. The decision of what names the individuals involved will use after marriage depends partly on the laws of the country in which the couple lives. Whether a woman chooses to adopt her husband's surname or keep her maiden name might be very important to her, if not in the first flush of married bliss then perhaps later when she finds her foreign surname a burden and perhaps an imposition. On the other hand, a surname that is normal in the majority society in which the couple live is a lot easier to use. It can be a great help in integrating as an immigrant if you have a majority language surname.

In some countries, it is possible for the woman to keep her own name and also acquire her husband's name, giving a double-barrelled variant, in which case the name, for example Una Cunningham-Andersson, gives a thumbnail sketch of the story of its bearer's life. Unfortunately this kind of name may have an upper-class ring to it in some parts of the English-speaking world. In other countries it is not the custom for women to change their name at all on marriage. Sometimes it is possible for the man to take the woman's surname on marriage, although this option tends not to be as popular. The couple must reach their own decision within the options available to them. In my own case, I used the name Una Cunningham-Andersson for the first 17 years of marriage, but changed my name officially back to Una Cunningham. Not only is it shorter and more convenient, the principle of taking a husband's name is simply less appealing to me now than it was when I was 25. This does not stop me from booking a table at a restaurant in the name of Andersson when that feels like an easier option than spelling Cunningham on the phone!

The question of what to name the children of intercultural marriages can be even more controversial. Fortunately it is usually possible to give a child two or even more forenames, so that both cultures are represented. The names given to the child may be chosen in accordance with this, giving combinations which may not go well together but serve the purpose of reflecting the child's background. An alternative is to give the child names which work in both languages: English, Swedish or Spanish speakers could name a child Maria or Daniel and have a name which looks native for all concerned when it is written, even if the pronunciation is somewhat different in each language. Parents often try to predict where they are likely to spend most of their time while the children are growing up and ensure that names are unremarkable in that country. Other parents might like to choose a name from the other culture, to give an unusual name in the country of residence. There are different ways of rationalising the difficult process of choosing names for children, and parents can only hope that their children will not hold their choice of name against them.

There are many advantages to ensuring that children have a reasonable and useful name, wherever they end up. One way to achieve this is to give them several names. Different countries will have different legislation about the number of names a child can be given and about which of them can be used to address the child. In Sweden you can give a child any number of names, but you will have to specify which of these is to be used to address the child, although this can later be changed fairly easily.

Our take on this was to give our children three names each – at least one that was very ordinary in Swedish, at least one that was very ordinary in English and a bonus name that was from one or other of our families. So far, our children have been happy to be called by the names we chose to address them by, except for Anders, who at the age of 12 chose to be known as John, his second name, at school. This has led to some confusion, since he continues to be known as Anders in the family, and the two worlds do sometimes meet. At the same time he changed his surname to mine, so that an exceptionally Swedish-sounding Anders Andersson became an unequivocally English language John Cunningham. The name John does exist with that spelling in Swedish, but with a different pronunciation.

We knew we were going to live in Mexico and gave our kids Spanish first names. This makes for a more comfortable environment for them.

(R. Chandler-Burns, Mexico)

Be prepared!

There are some aspects of parenthood in a bilingual family that may come as a surprise to those involved. For example, a parent speaking the minority language to a child is very conspicuous. It may be unpleasant at first to see heads turn when you say something to your child in the hearing of strangers. As long as the mixed language family is just a couple, then they probably do not attract much attention in public. Many immigrant parents find that they do not become conspicuous until they are out with their children. This is particularly so if the parent and child do not look 'foreign', for example a Dutch mother in Germany, a Finnish father in Norway, or a Spanish mother in Italy. To the casual onlooker it may then come as a surprise to hear that the parent and child speak another language. They 'look' as though they ought to speak German, Norwegian or Italian or whatever. If onlookers also get to know that the parent can actually speak the majority language perfectly well, it may seem absurd to be speaking another language to the child, particularly if the child is too little to understand much of what is being said. For most people foreign languages are difficult, and it may be quite incomprehensible to them that a tiny child can learn more than one language. This may lead to open criticism of the parent or unsolicited advice, which can be just as unpleasant:

> People (strangers) usually have two reactions when they hear me and the child speak English in public (how could I ever refrain myself and adopt another linguistic posture?). Most people will smile and attempt to say something like 'What's your name?' etc. and will ask if he understands Portuguese – so far, both mother and child are 'tolerated' because I do speak Portuguese and always stress that he understands Portuguese – which pleases people no end and somehow softens their (yes, occasional) attitude of 'these foreigners who think they can just walk about in our country without speaking Portuguese!' On other occasions people will 'marvel' at the child's ability to 'perform' in two languages, but I will always explain that children are like sponges and will learn anything given the opportunity.
> (Ana Cristina Gabriel, Lisbon)

> You will have people who are a bit annoyed because you have a language they don't understand. I would talk to my children in English and some people would come up to me and say, 'Why are you talking English to your children?' I said, 'Because I'm English,' and they said, 'But you're in Sweden now.' And English is a language

most people would understand. If someone speaks a language that isn't well known here people will react and the children will feel different. But you have to fight against it because eventually the children are going to love you for giving them a language.

(Loretta, Sweden)

In some families the children will hate the attention that the public use of the minority language generates, and will avoid the situation as much as possible. Others will not mind, or will even feel proud of their linguistic prowess. Of course, the level of attention will depend on the setting. In cosmopolitan areas it is not unusual to hear foreign languages. Passers-by in other places may make disparaging comments to the effect that 'When you're here speak ... ' There are two different perspectives in conflict here. On the one hand, some sensitive people may feel excluded and perhaps even feel that any conversation in a language they do not understand is probably about them. On the other hand, there is the feeling that anyone should be free to speak any language they please in any situation:

I know for a fact that my sons were embarrassed to speak English when they grew up. My daughter embraced it; she loved the idea of being different. But when I spoke English to my sons they did refuse for the first teenage years to speak English to me. ... Adolescence, together with 'I'm different' – it's tough!

(Loretta, Sweden)

There was one moment of crisis when my daughter, not long after she started school at the age of four, said to me in Spanish, 'Daddy don't speak to me in English in the street.' Ana is very shy and conscious of people looking at her. She didn't want to shine out. Now she's quite different. Now she is interested in my speaking to her in English.

(David, Spain)

In the case of parents trying to bring up a child as a speaker of a minority language, being able to speak the said language in all situations will be important. Obviously, the reaction to speaking a minority language in public will depend on several things:

• The listeners may not be used to hearing a foreign language spoken at all. While multicultural societies have become the norm in large parts of the industrial world, and while much of the developing world has always been multilingual, there are many places with a fairly monolingual population.

- They may have a generally negative attitude to all things foreign. This can be true of both people who live as part of the majority, or the most privileged group, in a multicultural society and those who live isolated from other groups.
- They may have a particularly negative attitude to speakers of the language in question. Regional, national and international tension and conflict, sometimes stretching far back in time, can create antipathy between groups, which has unfortunate consequences for those who live with a foot in each group.
- They may feel that they are being talked about. It is easy to misinterpret a conversation you do not understand.
- They may feel that visitors, and particularly immigrants, should learn and exclusively use the majority language, even with each other. In this case they might view it as particularly unsuitable to pass on the foreign language to a child. This has traditionally been the stance adopted in much of the world, where immigrants were expected to assimilate into the majority culture rather than integrate, bringing their language and culture with them.

Another, perhaps unexpected, aspect of new parenthood is that the parent who has to change from the language spoken by the couple to the language he or she is to speak to the child may be reluctant to do so, despite the plans laid down by the couple before the birth.

Examples

A Spanish man and French woman lived in Spain. They spoke the minority language, French, together. Before their child was born, they decided that they would each speak their own language to the child, in all situations. When the child was born, his father felt very strange switching from French to Spanish for the sake of a tiny baby who understood nothing he said. At the insistence of his wife, he persevered, and continued speaking Spanish to his son.

A Greek man and English woman living in England had much the same experience. The Greek man was to speak Greek to his daughter, but felt unable to switch to Greek, especially since he did not use Greek otherwise except with adult Greek speakers and in Greece. As a result, the child did not grow up speaking Greek, but her mother arranged for her to receive lessons in Greek from a private teacher from the age of six. She is now able to speak enough to communicate with her Greek grandmother. Her father has become more interested in speaking Greek to her.

In some cases a minority language may be the only clue that its speaker belongs to an oppressed or unpopular group. In such cases parents must decide how they and their children will use the languages. There are undoubtedly situations where discretion is required and where children need to learn that their minority language is not always viewed positively. For example, this situation is faced by American English speakers in certain parts of the Middle East or Kurdish speakers in countries with a Kurdish minority. Parents who succeed in helping their children to acquire the minority language in such circumstances are to be admired. In the years since September 2001, the position of Muslims and other peoples from the Middle East in the Western world has changed and this has led to difficulties for many people living in the West who wish to bring up their children as speakers of Arabic, Persian, Urdu, Pashto or any of a multitude of other languages spoken in that part of the world. Whether or not the family is Muslim they may meet negative attitudes, which in some cases lead to the parents choosing to speak the majority language in public, and maybe even at home. This will inevitably make it extremely difficult for the children to acquire the parents' language:

> 'Raising children bilingually' isn't so pretty when your home language is hated. Keeping your minority status isn't easy when you know it's going to cause your kids problems, and it's worse if your minority has ever been the object of genocide – the case of Indians, Jews, Gypsies and many others.
>
> (Anonymous, Mexico)

Reactions from the folk back home

The news that their grown-up son or daughter has 'taken up with a foreigner' might come as a shock to many parents, particularly if the son or daughter concerned lives in the home country. Even if the foreigner concerned is a fellow European and there is no major ethnic difference, the thought of the cultural and linguistic problems ahead may seem daunting. Many worry about their prospective grandchildren and wonder if such a relationship can ever be successful. They may wonder if they will be able to communicate with the boyfriend or girlfriend, and dread the prospect of their child moving to another country. Accepting a foreigner into the family is often a challenge for the older generation on both sides.

The extended family of cousins, grandparents, uncles and aunts on both sides may have mixed feelings about the family's way of dealing with the two languages they live with. On the one hand, the first child of the family may be watched closely for signs that this business of two languages is just too much to expect from a baby. On the other hand, the side or sides of the family representing the minority language (one or both sets of grandparents) may well be worried about not being able to communicate at all with their grandchildren if they do not learn to speak their language. If the children manage to learn enough of the minority language to build up a relationship with their grandparents, this will probably be appreciated, although some grandparents can be insensitive enough to criticise the children's hard-won skills as not being native-like.

This kind of remark can be hurtful to the parent who, often single-handed, helped the children acquire their minority language skills. Bear in mind that grandparents may be deeply disappointed that their son or daughter lives far away from them in another country; they may be unfamiliar with the culture and traditions of the country in which their child and grandchildren live. If their grandchildren's other parent is from that country, this can also be a source of sorrow to the grandparents:

> In trying to maintain a bilingual household, it has had an impact on my wife's family. They all think it is great!!! My mother-in-law, sister-in-law and brother-in-law have taken up Spanish.
>
> (Edgar Monterroso, USA)

> Our parents sometimes think we've done our children a disservice by raising them in a second culture and language.
>
> (Joyce Roth, Japan)

If the majority language spoken in the country where the children live is a high prestige language, especially if it is a school language for children in the country where the minority language is spoken, such as French is in England, and English is in Sweden, the emigrant parent may come upon envy from his or her own siblings, who feel that their children are not being given such an advantageous upbringing, with the chance to acquire a second language with what looks like no effort at all. Their children will instead have to learn the 'hard' way, at school, with grammar exercises and vocabulary lists, with presumably less chance of success. The work put into living with two languages, by parents and children alike, is not immediately observable from the outside.

The best case is a situation where grandparents and other family members support and try to understand the targets and efforts of the family with two or more languages. The role of minority language-speaking extended family is important. As the child grows, they will be an important resource in providing input in the minority languages. They can also be an invaluable source of minority language materials, and for older children they can offer an environment for perfecting heritage language skills while learning about their cultural background.

Chapter 3

The family language system

Developing a system

According to their circumstances, a family will develop a system regulating the use of the two languages with which they live. When the circumstances change in some way, the system must be flexible enough to meet the requirements made of it. When a mixed language couple first meet they will decide actively, or by default, which language to speak. As time goes on, that decision might need revising; perhaps another solution becomes more appropriate when a child is born, or when the child needs help with majority language homework. A divorce, moving to another country or the arrival of a new member of the family (maybe granny moves in) might require changes in the family's language set-up. A family which has chosen for both parents to use the minority language at home might want to reconsider this decision if they move to a country where that language is the majority language. Then the former majority language needs a place in which it is spoken if it is to be kept alive. Of course, if neither parent is a native speaker of that language they may have no need or wish to keep up their own or their children's skills in the language.

Example

A family with a Swedish father and an American mother lived for many years in Sweden, where both the mother and father spoke English at home to the children. Outside the home the father spoke his native Swedish to the children, while the mother continued to speak English to the children in all situations. When the family went to live in the USA for two years, they needed to ensure that the children's Swedish was kept up, both for the sake of their communication with their Swedish relatives and since they knew they would be returning after two years. They tried to switch to everybody speaking Swedish at home, but it did not work, for two reasons. First, the mother did not feel comfortable speaking Swedish to the children at all: she had never done so and her Swedish (which had never been that good) was rapidly weakening while away from Sweden. Second, the father was required to work long hours and was often away from home from early morning to late evening, and he rarely saw his children during the week. He was not around to speak Swedish to either his wife or his children. The result was that by the time the family moved back to Sweden the children were monolingual in English, and seemed to have forgotten all the Swedish they had ever known. Fortunately, it gradually came back to them once they got back to school and got into the way of things Swedish again. Now the children are very competent in both languages.

The language chosen by brothers and sisters to talk between themselves is usually the majority language if this is their dominant language (as is usual, at least for children of school age). Sometimes parents may try to persuade their children to talk in the minority language together, but it is difficult to influence others' choice of language, and in any case it is not really any of the parents' business. It may be that the minority language has a greater chance of being used between siblings if it is the only language spoken by both parents at home, but even this is not always any help.

Well, at home we were raised speaking Catalan to my ma and Spanish to my da and then we would speak Spanish among us four sisters. So sitting at the table we would use both depending on the contents of the conversation and who you were mainly addressing your questions or attention to. And then, of course, Catalan to my grandparents.

(Pilar, raised with Spanish and Catalan
in Catalonia)

My brother moved to Florida when he was 25 and then had very little contact with my parents. By then he started speaking English of course. Now he has moved back to Sweden, and we speak Swedish together. He manages to speak Danish to my mother but for us it seems more natural now to speak Swedish. When we were children we spoke Danish together, until he moved. I think it's because his Danish is not as good as it was, so I think we can express ourselves better if we speak Swedish together. Now he has a Swedish wife, so it is natural.

(Pia, raised with Danish at home in Sweden)

Sometimes older siblings address a younger one in the minority language if they believe it might get better results (perhaps sounding more authoritative, i.e. more like Mum or Dad) or if they perceive the younger child as understanding the minority language better (which may well be the case).

Example

Leif (9;5) to Patrik (3;10): 'Ge mig den Pat, give it to me!'

Language and personality

It is an unavoidable fact of life with two languages that everyone in the family who speaks the minority language also sometimes has to speak the majority language, unless the family lives in a self-contained ex-pat or immigrant environment. Even parents who always speak the minority language in all situations when speaking directly to their children will sometimes have to use the majority language to others in the presence of their children. For small children it can be confusing to hear a parent change languages when talking, say, to a shop assistant. So much alters when we switch languages: some languages are spoken in a higher tone of voice than others; the amount of pitch movement may change; a speaker might speak with lower volume in one language than another, for cultural reasons or because of uncertainty, which can make the speaker appear less self-assured. It may seem to small children that their parents alter their personality when they change language, particularly if they are not used to hearing them do so.

In fact, some aspects of a speaker's personality do seem to change when switching from a native language to a non-native language. In a language which is not completely mastered, speakers do not have access to stylistic variation and nuances of meaning:

> She used both bad English and Italian, whichever language was easier to express herself in. And of course, being of a passionate nature, whenever she got slightly angry, slightly happy, slightly sad, then the Italian would come rushing out, because she didn't have the linguistic capability to express those feelings in English.
> (Loretta, raised with Italian and English)

Speech may become hesitant and uncertain, which gives the impression that speakers are unsure about what they are saying. It is difficult to win an argument elegantly in a second language. This is an important reason why parents need to think carefully before giving up their own language when talking to their children. They are likely to lose prestige in the eyes of their children if they are not fully competent in the language they use to speak to them. Ultimately this may lead to a lack of respect, which might have been avoided if parents had been able to stick to their own language in all dealings with their children.

Parents with two languages

People who have grown up with two languages may want to pass both languages on to their children. This may not be altogether easy, depending on the family's make-up and circumstances. A young man who grew up in, say, Spain with an English mother and a Spanish father will probably speak much more native-like Spanish than English. If he marries a Spanish woman and they make their home in Spain, he may want his children to learn his second language, English. His mother may be very keen to help, not wanting to have to speak Spanish to her grandchildren. There may, however, be difficulties if he does not feel confident enough speaking English to his children. In addition, his Spanish wife may not be in favour of introducing a second language at all, not really perceiving her husband as anything but a Spaniard.

Whether this kind of arrangement works out depends on how motivated the parents are to help their children learn the minority language. If the children are to achieve a reasonable degree of proficiency, steps must be taken to ensure that they are exposed to the language frequently, either through their grandparents or other people:

> I have children and grandchildren. I brought them up in one language only – Hebrew. Although my husband and I occasionally speak Dutch, we did not think this was an important language, and thus decided not to teach our children Dutch. However, I did think of the importance of English, but my husband was not very good at English, so it would have been 'artificial' if we had spoken English together.
>
> (Yedida Heymans, Israel)

> Any children of ours would grow up multilingual too. My husband, in spite of being American, also speaks Korean, and has picked up a fair number of Dutch words and phrases and some Farsi through contact with my parents. We would probably talk to them in the

same linguistic hodge-podge I had growing up; I know from
personal experience that children can sort it out and limit the
domain of each when necessary.

(Jasmin Harvey, USA)

Of course, not everyone shares this opinion:

> As a translator, I know how difficult it is to speak one's mother
> tongue properly, how the language constantly evolves (my five-
> year-old dictionary has become obsolete), and how important it is
> to give a child the proper tools to learn to appreciate his mother
> tongue, the richness and the classics of it, before he decides to learn
> another language. If you impose on the child another language, he
> will not have the time (or he will lose the desire) to explore his
> mother tongue. Twenty-four hours in a day, less eight hours' sleep,
> less eating and playing with other kids … I mean, give the poor kid
> a break. The real issue is: what is better? To really learn and explore
> one language, or to approximately communicate in two?
>
> (Jacques Clau, Canada)

One person–one language

For many years the one person–one language (OPOL) method of raising
children bilingually has been recommended to mixed language couples
as the most suitable. The main principle is that the parents each speak
their own language to their children. The children are then expected to
answer their parents in the language the parents use to them. For some
parents this is the only conceivable way to manage the situation. If
neither parent is prepared to surrender the privilege of speaking their
language to their child, then this is the way to go about life in a mixed
language family. There are, however, potential problems with this
method. If the parent who represents the minority language is not with
the children much, they may not get enough input in this language.
This may lead to them never really getting started with the minority
language:

> My idea then was that the OPOL method was the best from what
> I had heard, so we decided that I would speak French to Alienor
> and Wendy would speak Chinese to her. What we had not fig-
> ured, though, was that the little time I could spend with Alienor
> would not be enough for her to get a fair dose of French. I must
> say that I have a full-time job with long hours and that on top of

that I work two or three weekends a month on freelance translations, which does keep me busy. When I have some free time, the
first thing that comes to my mind is to relax, and interacting in
French with my children when they don't always understand what
I say sometimes does not feel very relaxing to me.

(Alain Fontaine, Taiwan)

An additional problem may arise with the one person–one language
method if the parents do not both understand the other's language. It is
possible to feel quite left out of conversations between the child and the
other parent if you do not understand what they are saying. One solution
to this problem is for each parent to improve their knowledge of the
other parent's language. There will otherwise be difficulties when the
family is assembled. These can be overcome if the parents are determined
to make the system work:

The situation was that my father is Czech, my mum is Iranian and
I grew up in Scotland. My parents talk to each other in English,
but neither speaks the other language well at all. I think it was my
father who was the driving force. He insisted that each parent speak
their native language to us. I think mum was a bit less draconian.
Dad was quite strict on it. Each of them talked to us in their language, Farsi and Czech, and I think that initially, when I went to
school for the first time, my English wasn't that good. My first two
languages were Czech and Farsi. That went on through childhood.
Even now I talk to my parents in their languages. They insisted that
communication would be in the language of the parent.

(Adam, Farsi, Czech and English
in Scotland)

If the parents do understand each other's language, then it is possible for
one of them to pick up a conversational thread started by the other,
switching languages as they go:

LEIF (9;7): 'I want to go to town soon.'
MOTHER: 'We'll be going sometime this week.'
FATHER: 'Vad vill du göra dar?' ('What do you want to do there?')

The one person–one language method requires that the speaker
establishes contact with the appropriate listener before beginning to
speak. It is not really possible to make a remark intended for both parents, although children must, of course, sometimes find a way round

that problem. Our experience is that the children ensure that the appropriate parent is listening before starting to say what they want to, by first saying 'Mamma!' or 'Pappa!' and waiting for an answer. If the remark is intended for both parents they will sometimes check the other parent's attention and understanding by asking a follow-on question of that parent.

Suzanne Romaine (1995: 186) writes that a very common outcome of the one person–one language method is children who can understand the languages of both parents but speak only the language of the community in which they live. She goes on to say that sociolinguistic studies have shown that it is very difficult for children to acquire active command of a minority language where that language does not receive support from the community. Arnberg (1987: 35–42) confirms this with the results of a study of Swedish–English-speaking children in Sweden who by the age of seven would all answer their English-speaking mothers in Swedish. The children were, however, able to converse in English when motivated to do so; they were willing to speak English to the experimenter. The parents expressed disappointment at their children's lack of fluency in English. In some cases, children may even begin to avoid the parent who speaks their weaker language with them:

> At the moment my daughter prefers to be spoken to in English. Sometimes I am very tempted to use English because she seems to respond much better to English. Whenever both of us go to pick our daughter up from the childcare she wants to go straight to my husband and absolutely refuses to come to me. We are not sure why. Some say because girls often like fathers more. We suspect that the fact I speak Japanese to her may cause this reaction. She might not like to be spoken to in Japanese. Even at home she wants to be with him rather than with me. Especially when she is tired.
>
> (Kaori Matsuda, Australia)

> Prior to kindergarten, we spoke English with them, but of course they picked up Japanese from their playmates. After entering kindergarten, the balance of Japanese/English shifted to Japanese. I spoke Japanese with the children because that's the more difficult one and they needed help with school. My husband's Japanese wasn't very good, so the children tended to avoid speaking with him when they were primary age.
>
> (Joyce Roth, Japan)

There are, however, success stories, such as those reported in Saunders (1982) and Dopke (1992). Romaine (1995) comments that the success stories concern minority languages which are not stigmatised and children from an advantaged background. Arnberg (1987: 43) points out that most studies of successful bilingualism are made by linguists concerning their own children. Saunders (1988: 33) rejects the notion that only middle-class families can succeed in raising children with two languages, offering evidence from a study he has made concerning a Turkish labourer who successfully raised his two daughters in Australia as competent Turkish/English bilinguals (Saunders 1984).

But while there is in many European countries a close relationship between a single national language and a nation state, this is certainly not the case everywhere. Indeed the experiences of families in many parts of the world, such as in South Asia and Africa, where knowledge of multiple languages is the norm, suggest that neither an advantaged background nor belonging to the middle class is necessary for success in raising children with multiple languages. In addition to developing proficiency in a number of indigenous languages, children in these countries are often educated in English-medium schools:

> I didn't grow up with my parents. They lived in Lagos, so I lived with my grandparents. They spoke Igbo with me. When I was young Igbo was the only language I knew – that was my language. But my mum spoke Yoruba also, and my grandmother spoke Hausa. But I wasn't able to learn that one. They are not at all related. Igbo is different from Yoruba and different from Hausa. When you move to another part of Nigeria you are forced to learn the language also so as to integrate yourself into society. Usually when you grow up in the environment you just pick it up.
>
> (Anonymous, from Nigeria)

> There was a mix of languages when I was brought up. To me, my parents spoke Pashto usually, and Hindko to each other, but we could understand what they were saying. After the age of four or five I went to school and in school it was our national language, which is Urdu. ... My parents came to the Punjab and the common language of the south province was Punjabi. ... I was also used to speaking this, not in my early years, but from eight to 10 years when I was out with other children I would speak Punjabi.
>
> (Nazir, from Pakistan)

My own personal experience, as a parent, of the one person–one
language method is very positive. Our children are in their teens and
twenties now, and their own take on their linguistic childhood is presented in Chapter 10. They were spoken to in the minority language,
English, by their mother and in the majority language, Swedish, by their
father. All of them will now always answer in the language in which they
are addressed, and their English is no longer laced with Swedish words,
although Anders and Patrik report using more English in their Swedish
than is usual among their peers. (It has to be said that many young Swedes
enjoy incorporating English words and phrases into their Swedish.) They
can and will speak more careful English to monolingual English speakers,
just like the children in Arnberg's work. Leif and Anders have studied in
Scotland and England, respectively, and while they were treated as European students among others, they had considerably better proficiency
than other Swedish students. Leif's ease and skills far exceed those of his
monolingual peers. His Swedish is native. Anders has, from about the age
of seven, been very particular about keeping the languages separate,
sometimes asking for vocabulary before he starts speaking. At 14;10, his
English vocabulary had no obvious gaps. He attended English-medium
schools from the age of 12 and that enabled his English to develop to a
point where he can be described as native-like in both languages. In fact,
subtle phonetic measurements suggest that he appeared at age 14 to be
dominant in English (Cunningham 2003). Patrik went through monolingual phases. At age four he spoke almost only English, although he
understood Swedish well. At 6;5 he spoke only Swedish, although he
understood English as well as Swedish. At 11;0 he used the languages
appropriately, answering in English when addressed in English, although
his English syntax and pronunciation were not native-like. His Swedish
was native. Now at the age of 18 his Swedish is exceptionally well
developed and his English is very nearly native-like. In Chapter 10 you
can read Patrik's own account of this. Lisa attended a bilingual (English/
Swedish) class from the age of seven to 10 and now at 16 appears to be
well balanced in her languages, as she was already at the age of nine
(Cunningham 2003), and indeed to have native-like skills for her age in
both languages. The children were all English-dominant until they started
pre-school at around three years of age. They all had a period of Swedish
dominance when they started pre-school and school, and for Lisa and
Anders that has changed since they entered bilingual or English-medium
schooling, leaving them native-like in both languages.

I think the advantage is that the child(ren) can associate one language system to one parent and can sort two languages out in their

mind in early stages of their life. Disadvantage is that I (or my husband) have to be rude to our guests who are monolingual. Even in public (such as in shops, childcare, etc.) I sometimes feel slightly awkward speaking in the minority language.

(Kaori Matsuda, Australia)

I never spoke English with my kids — I was very principled about that aspect of the learning process.

(Andreas Schramm, Minnesota)

When our second child was learning to talk, she used to look at a new person, put her hands on her head and say, 'Head.' If she didn't get a response, she would say, 'Huvud.' Usually people would respond with hands, feet, tummy. It was her way of screening what language she should try with them.

(American mother in Sweden)

Every person should speak always only one (and the same) language with the children when they are very young. (I have heard about children growing up with three or four languages if they can associate a determinate person with a determinate language.) Another important thing is to have at least two adults speaking the 'minority' language with the child and between themselves. After discussing these problems with other bilingual families we came to the conclusion that the child needs to hear 'a dialogue'. Perhaps this is the reason my children never refused to speak Slovak in public, as often happens. My mother used to stay with us for long periods and we also spent our holidays in Slovakia.

(Elena Bertoncini, Italy)

My expectations have been met, and exceeded. My daughter can switch back and forth between French and English with ease and speed. I'm satisfied with how bilingualism is working within our family.

(Leslie Yee, Canada)

The one parent–one language method usually means that the child is introduced to both languages from birth. Some parents and others feel that two languages at once is too much for a tiny baby to deal with. They are afraid that the child will end up completely confused, without real competence in either language. These fears may be fuelled by observing young children at a certain stage of bilingual development who freely mix the languages, and even older children who mix the languages in certain circumstances. However, young children, despite a period of confusion and maybe even frustration, seem to get it all sorted out if they get enough input in both languages, even if the parents are not especially consistent. The older children learn that they can mix the languages for ease of communication or for effect with others who share their linguistic background, but they soon learn to keep the languages 'pure' when around monolinguals, at least at the lexical (word) level, even if they still have interference from the majority language in the grammar and pronunciation of the minority language.

Unfortunately, there are cases where parents are advised that bilingualism is not good for their child. This view is based on some very early studies which have since been thoroughly discredited. This is discussed further in Chapter 11. These parents may choose not to speak the minority language at all, planning to introduce it later, when the child has become competent in the majority language. The problem with this plan is that it is very difficult to change the language you use to speak to a person, and older children are not likely to appreciate being spoken to in a language they do not understand; they will have to be 'taught' the language first. It is much easier with tiny babies, who do not expect to understand what they hear.

Some families may choose not to speak their language with their children because they wish the child to become assimilated totally in the majority culture. This was, for example, the case in the large-scale migration from Europe to the United States in the nineteenth and early twentieth centuries, where many people switched to English as soon as they could. Even in Europe, parents were often advised not to speak their own language to their children. It is now generally thought that this advice was misguided. Children can manage very well with the majority language if they just get enough input from native speakers. If a lot of their majority language input is from non-native speakers, they may have influences from those speakers in their majority language speech. In addition, older children may come to feel ashamed of or look down on their parents if they speak the majority language poorly, especially if that is the language the parents use with the children. It is a shame to deny children access to their parents' language and culture. Later in life the children will perhaps lament never having learned their parents' language, and may feel cut off from part of their heritage:

> I have strong views about bilingualism. It is really important that both languages are allowed to be part of the child's life. You can't just think, okay, she speaks Swedish in school so it doesn't matter if

she loses her Arabic, for example. It is important to keep it. It's part of her identity anyhow. If she loses it she will miss it when she's a teenager, like I did with Serbian, and I was really sad and disappointed in my parents that they hadn't kept it up for me. I felt I'd lost part of my identity because I felt that Montenegro was part of me and I was sad that I didn't know the language as well as I wanted to. So I speak Swedish with my daughter, but my husband speaks Arabic.

(Alexandra, Sweden)

It happens fairly often in mixed language families that the parents start off each speaking their own languages to the children but eventually drift into using the majority language together. This seems to be more likely to happen if the parents use the majority language when speaking to each other, so that the minority language parent only has to shift into that language to speak to the children. If the children go through a stage (temporary or permanent) of answering the minority language parent in the majority language it is easy to go on in that language, which is the children's dominant language. The parent may then give up what feels like an uphill struggle to impose a language on reluctant children, and stop using the minority language altogether or use it sporadically. This result can feel like a failure all round. If it is at all possible, it may be better to carry on using the minority language to the children, even if they respond in the majority language: they will be learning passive skills just by listening, and passive knowledge of a language can easily become active on a trip to a country where the language is spoken:

My mother spoke Serbian and switched between Serbian and Swedish. I noticed that she used more and more Swedish for every year that passed. So when we were really young, she spoke mostly Serbian – seldom Swedish – with us. Through the years, as we became teenagers, Swedish was more dominant. I suppose we didn't use Serbian any more, so my mother was only used to Swedish.

(Alexandra, Sweden)

When I remind her to ask her mother for the word she needs, she's willing to continue in Portuguese thereafter. I think my wife didn't expect that she'd have to police Isis' speech, and she tends not to do so, so it's up to me to remind them both of the rule. So, I guess

I wish Isis' bilingualism weren't another place for me to be the family's main disciplinarian.

(Don Davis, Boston)

I would prefer my kids to speak German back to me all the time. But when we travel to Germany, all children tend to switch to German easily if necessary after a short time (two to five days). ... I was hoping for a more balanced situation but understand why that cannot be, given the circumstances. I still wish my kids would speak more German with me, but I am happy that my eight-year-old middle child is doing a fair amount of it with me.

(Andreas Schramm, Minnesota)

Most people assume that it is easiest to speak your native language, but this is not always so. I conduct my life in Hebrew (except when I am in the classroom, teaching English), and although I may express myself more clearly and in a more sophisticated manner in English, I often find it easier to speak Hebrew. Often when I am tired I just don't have the strength to speak English to my children. I know that this is not the way it should be (I believe that a parent should be consistent about the language he/she uses), but it is the truth. I know many English speakers who have never spoken English with their children for this exact reason.

(Bari Nirenberg, Israel)

Some immigrant parents end up using the majority language with their children because they have monolingual majority language speakers in the house. An immigrant mother who works, for example, as a childminder will not be able to speak her language freely to her child without making her other charges feel left out. Faced with the choice between saying everything twice and switching to the majority language when the other children are present, it is easy to understand how the majority language can take over:

Yesterday Freddy was at my sister's house for a couple of hours alone. When I went to pick him up I spoke to him in English in their presence, but it did seem false to me. I wonder if Freddy notices. Similarly, I brought him in to my office last week and in front of the others here spoke to him in English. Naturally, he doesn't really respond to me when I speak to him in English. It's all for the comfort of the others – the politeness factor.

(Margo Miller, USA)

Let me say that, at times and in certain situations, it would be impolite to those around us to speak English in public. People might think we're either being snooty or trying to 'talk behind their back' to their face. It's a problem at parties sometimes. So you talk Spanish.

(Harold Ormsby, Mexico)

Before I would switch to English so as to not exclude anyone. Now I don't care how they feel. My relationship with my son is most important to me.

(Dr Edgar Monterroso, USA)

When we had German guests, however, my husband spoke German to them, but still spoke Dutch to the children, which always annoyed me because I considered it rude, especially as I was always asked to translate. Still, the system worked very well.

(Gabriele Kahn, Oregon)

At one stage our son complained when someone used the non-expected language, just as has been reported in the literature. He has now stopped doing this, perhaps because of growing meta-linguistic awareness: if he can use two languages, why shouldn't other people?

(Steve Matthews, Hong Kong)

One language—one location (minority language at home)

Parents with different native languages who are concerned that the minority language will not get enough input if it is heard only from one parent may choose the one language—one location model, whereby both parents speak the minority language at home to their children. This method is also usually chosen by families where both parents are native speakers of the minority language. This may mean that children meet the majority language for the first time in the neighbourhood play park or when they start at pre-school or school. Fortunately children are generally very motivated to learn the language they need to communicate, and they usually manage very well when they start meeting monolingual majority language speakers. This model is particularly appropriate where the minority language receives little or no support in the community. In such a case the language will need all the input it can get; even the input from a parent for whom it is not a native language can be valuable. Purists might, however, reject the idea of parents speaking any language other than their native language to their children:

> I am a Chicana [a person of Mexican descent living in the USA]. As such I was raised by monolingual Spanish-speaking parents in Los Angeles. My first contact with English occurred in kindergarten and by first grade no other language was accepted by my teachers. This literally meant that unless I asked to go to the toilet in English, I wasn't allowed to go.
>
> (Anonymous, USA)

> My husband, although American, loves to speak German, and so we all speak German at home. If we didn't, the children might lose the language altogether because they even speak English to each other now most of the time. I know lots of adults here who came to the country as children and totally lost their first language. I always find it hard to imagine when people tell me, 'My parents spoke German at home, but I don't speak it.'
>
> (Gabriele Kahn, Oregon)

> I do understand the concern about wanting the child to speak the kindergarten language (usually majority language) before he enters it. However, I think that at that age (about two and a half or three, I suppose, as it is here in Belgium), the children are pretty able to pick up that new language, especially for that one, because they will be exposed to it most of the day. Before entering kindergarten, I only spoke Spanish and German. The majority language here is French, so I entered kindergarten in French, without knowing a single word of it. My mother tells me that French reached the level of both other languages in a few months. Now French has become my major language. I would rather have concern for the minority language from the start. It's that language that will have to be defended and improved later on. The exposure to majority language will be such that I wouldn't worry for that before kindergarten. Unfortunately, my wife doesn't speak German, so we can't switch to full German exposure at home. I think I would have done it to increase the German influence in our French environment.
>
> (Alfred Wiesen, Belgium)

> I have come to the conclusion that there is little or no need to expose children to the majority language in the home. We moved

to Japan when our oldest (and at that time only) child, Francis, was about seven months old. Since my wife's (non-native) English is fluent, we began with a policy of 100 per cent English at home, with exceptions for socialisation with Japanese speakers. At the time we reasoned that he would get enough exposure to Japanese outside the home, especially once he started school, so we should emphasise English at home in order to maximise the opportunity to become truly bilingual. Anyway, we were satisfied with our English home until Francis was three. Then we noticed that he was becoming more shy with neighbourhood playmates. We feared it might be because his Japanese progress was lagging behind that of his peers, so my wife began speaking Japanese to him during the day while I was at work, with everyone switching to English when I was at home. The change in Francis was dramatic. Within a couple of months we felt his Japanese had caught up with that of his monolingual friends and his shyness had eased to what we felt was a more healthy level. However, the pendulum did not stop in the middle but has continued on its arc. Our initial opinion about exposure to Japanese at school has proven correct. Francis speaks excellent native Japanese with a strong Osaka accent (though some Japanese might argue that an Osaka accent is anathema to excellence). Our concern now is that at home he has been showing an increasing preference to speak Japanese and a corresponding reluctance to use English. We recently decided that my wife should try to go back to using English during the day, both to encourage Francis to practise and for the sake of our younger children. In retrospect, I think we may have over-reacted when Francis was three. We have now seen a little more of all the different 'problem' stages that children go through and get over before long without any permanent damage. It also happens that his shy period was just after the birth of our second child, and that can certainly be a little stressful for any older sibling. In conclusion, I would recommend to parents in similar situations to start with the 100 per cent minority language home policy and stick with it, as long as there are opportunities for the children to socialise with majority language peers and decent majority language schools. The children will pick up the majority language just fine. (With us, the jury's still out on the minority language.)

(David Meyer, Japan)

Even in a home where both parents speak the minority language to the children and to each other, and the children answer the parents in that language, the children may speak the majority language between themselves. While this may be disturbing for the parents and seem to upset the minority language only policy that the parents are trying to implement, there is probably little that can be done about it. The relationship between siblings is private and really nothing to do with the parents.

Whether the parents in a mixed language family choose the one person—one language method or the one location—one language method will partly depend on how well they speak each other's languages. If they are both fluent in the minority language, then they may decide to use that language at home. If the majority language parent can understand the minority language but does not speak it well enough to use it with the children, or if the parents feel that they should each speak their own language to the children right from the word go, then the one person—one language method should be chosen.

'Artificial' bilingualism

It may seem unfair to monolingual couples that they do not have any natural way to give their children what many perceive to be the 'gift' of two languages. There are, however, families who go to extraordinary lengths to arrange for their children to grow up with two languages. Perhaps the most extreme method is simply to uproot the family and move to another country. This places not only the children but also the parents in a situation where they will be exposed to and need to learn a second language. Many European academics view a year or two spent at an American university not only as a step up their own career ladders, but also as a way to give their children a head start in English (and incidentally improve their own English).

A less drastic method is to let the children attend an international school or kindergarten if such an option is available locally. These schools offer education in all subjects through the medium of a language other than the majority language (often English or French). In some cases these schools are intended for pupils who already speak the language of instruction, but there are some cases where schools offer immersion education for beginners, either as a group or together with children who already know the language. Such schools operate in Canada, for example, where French-speaking children are put in English-speaking environments and vice versa, the aim being to give them two languages (see, e.g., Swain and Lapkin 1982), and in bilingual parts of Finland, where Swedish-speaking and Finnish-speaking children are given the chance to learn each other's language. Similarly, 'American' schools and 'English' schools can be found all over Europe, from Nicosia to Stockholm. Students at these schools often do very well indeed.

In multilingual situations, such as the cosmopolitan cities of Geneva or Brussels, parents are faced with many choices regarding their children's linguistic development. Couples working for one of the international organisations which have their headquarters in those cities are often mixed, each speaking their own language; in the cities more than one language is heard all round, and many friends and colleagues speak other languages. The school situation reflects the multilingual nature of the city:

> I live in Brussels and am bilingual Danish–English. My wife is Italian. My kids are growing up quadrilingual Italian, Danish, English, French. And there are huge communities here of similarly mixed/confusing situations.
>
> (Ian Bo Andersen, Brussels)

> It is absolutely necessary for the parents to decide which language they feel the child should dominate for their future and that is the language in which s/he (maybe particularly he, because it is my impression that little girls are often more verbal than little boys) should be schooled – still of course continuing to communicate with a child in other languages which are natural to the family – because after all the spoken language is much less rich in vocabulary, grammar, etc. than the written language. This was a big decision for many of the multicultural families at the UN because it was becoming increasingly evident that English was the most important language in the world, and why deprive a child of learning it as a dominant rather than a second language when there was the opportunity to do so?
>
> (Peggy Orchowski, California)

Another way to create a situation where children might naturally come to be exposed to two languages is to employ a foreign au pair to look after the children, or to place them with an immigrant child-minder who is a native speaker of the language the parents wish the child to acquire. If this option is not available, some monolingual majority language parents enrol their children in foreign language 'lessons' which are suitable for their age group. These lessons usually teach simple games and songs to the children and may help them to minimise their foreign accent if they eventually start learning the same language at school. Unfortunately these kinds of classes are sometimes held by non-native speakers of the language in question. It is, unfortunately, just as easy for young children to acquire, say, French with an English accent as with a native-like pronunciation.

There are some ambitious parents who embark on the mission of giving their children a second language which is neither parent's native language. This can be done either with the one person–one language method, whereby only one of the parents speaks the minority language with the children, or by the one location–one language method if both the parents decide to speak the minority language at home. Parents who decide to give their child two languages in this way are usually very motivated, which is a prerequisite for this kind of venture. George Saunders (1982, 1988) describes how he and his wife raised their children bilingually in German and English in Australia, although they were both English speakers from monolingual backgrounds. They had both studied German and lived in Germany and believed that bilingualism would have a positive effect on their children's lives. By all accounts Saunders and his wife were very successful, and managed to give their children a good level of German. His 1988 book is a very readable account of their experiences. Another way is that exemplified in the following extraordinary account:

All members of my family shared a first language, Finnish. There was no urgent need for us to become multilingual, but my parents had the original idea that my brother and I should be free of emotional ties to a single culture, so that we could choose where we wanted to live. With this end in mind, they wanted us to learn English. They encouraged me to learn to read Finnish quickly by promising me a wristwatch, which I earned by learning to read by age five. Then we began studying English, as a family, using a course called 'English by the Nature Method' (I think). The course consisted of texts given in conventional spelling and then in IPA [International Phonetic Alphabet] below each line. The texts also came on audiotape. It took us about four years of daily study to finish the course. (In retrospect, I realise this is somewhat unusual, but as a child I didn't know other people didn't go about things this way. As far as I remember, I thought it was fun to learn English.) So, when I was about nine, my parents told us that we were to stop speaking Finnish and use just English at home. I felt very threatened, but my parents assured me that I would not forget how to speak Finnish (they weren't really quite right about that, but oh, well) and I adjusted. We were speaking English in a non-English-speaking environment, with no input from native speakers, except for BBC broadcasts and occasional visits with British friends of the family. As a result, my family developed a home-grown variety of English, which, in retrospect, seems like a very bad idea. However, I came to the USA (at age 19) and was able to pick up native-like pronunciation and pragmatics (people don't necessarily notice that I'm not a native speaker of English) so I guess it turned out okay.

(Mai Kuha, USA)

Chapter 4

Language development

In the first five years of life the vast majority of children become proficient speakers of their first language. This is a remarkable achievement. Although each child is an individual, and will acquire language at his or her own pace, there are certain stages that all normally developing children pass through.

The first of these stages is the preparatory stage. During their first year, children learn to recognise a number of words. This might not seem much; after all, a dog can recognise a number of words too, but the young child has accomplished a great deal more during her first year. She has moved from being able to distinguish between the sounds of any of the world's languages to being able to ignore differences between sounds that are not used in the language or languages spoken to her. She will have been training her speech organs by babbling – practising the sounds of language and different kinds of intonation patterns. She has also developed her body language and uses it together with intonation so that those around her are seldom unsure about how she feels or what she wants.

Around the end of the child's first year or the beginning of the second year, he will have begun to produce a few words. Initially the words are produced in isolation, or together with babble. When a young child's own language production gets going, things move fast. By the end of the second year the child will usually have begun stringing words together and be very good at making his wishes known, even without using words. You can get a long way with gesture and intonation if your listener is interested in what you want to say!

From this stage on there is no stopping the child. The child's vocabulary expands extremely rapidly and the grammar of the language or languages the child is learning is fleshed out as the child's language tests the patterns he observes to see how to put words together. Linguists are still arguing about whether children growing up with two languages initially develop one system or two – that is, if they have a single set of rules to organise the way they produce language or if they have one set for each language they use. This topic is explored in more detail in Chapter 11.

Children who are born into mixed language or immigrant families have an early language development which is in many ways different from that experienced by those born into monolingual majority language families. In the case of mixed language families, where both languages are used at home, the child's main difficulty is caused by the relatively small amount of input in each language. Where monolingual English babies hear both parents saying the same words to them, as in 'Here's your teddy', 'Where's teddy now?', 'What a nice teddy!', children whose parents speak different languages to them will get less input in each language. If parents do not spend equal amounts of time talking to their children, which is the way things work out in most families, there will be little chance for the children to learn the words of one of the languages. The children are going to have a harder time separating the stream of sound into meaningful chunks of language than if they had only one language, because they will hear the same words being repeated less frequently.

Each object having two names is a source of sorrow to some children. Imagine the disappointment felt by the one-year-old who runs excitedly to her mother saying, 'Sko, sko!' with her new shoe in her hand only to be told, 'Well, actually, mummy says shoe,' or even worse, 'No, it's a shoe.' Perhaps the best thing to say in these circumstances is 'Yes, there's your shoe!' Obviously, great tact is required to help the child realise what is going on: that there are, in fact, two quite separate systems at work here. What the child says is correct, but inappropriate. These children have a lot more to learn than monolingual children.

Consistency on the part of the parents is probably very helpful in the early stages, that is, each parent using a single language when speaking directly to the child and, if possible, not changing according to who else is present. Families find many ways to accommodate their languages, and generally establish unwritten rules about who speaks which language to whom in which circumstances. There is a lot to be said for the one person–one language method, whereby each parent speaks their own language to the child come what may. Then the child can associate the words of each language with the appropriate parent. Another common solution is that the minority language is used in the home and the majority language used outside. For children under two or three it may be better for the parents to go on speaking the minority language even outside the home, just to help them organise their languages. The most important thing is to find an arrangement that suits everybody in the family. Children usually manage to adapt to whatever system the adults decide on, and can generally cope even with inconsistency in the long run:

> Usually it's all right. I can personally switch language fine between English and Swedish. At a parent–teacher meeting I can speak to my mother in English and then to my teachers in Swedish. But it feels more awkward if my teachers speak English. It doesn't matter which person he or she is speaking to. I don't feel comfortable if people outside my English-speaking world speak English to me.
>
> (Patrik, 18;0)

Around the age of two or three, many children who have been brought up with the one person–one language method will have achieved a level of metalinguistic awareness, i.e. they are able to talk about their languages and say things like 'Mummy says "dress", daddy says "klän-ning".' The child at this stage is aware that there are two systems, and will often try to keep the development of vocabulary in step, so that a new word in one language will soon be matched by the corresponding word in the other language. The mother can hold up an object and ask the child, 'What's this?' If the child knows the right word, she will give the word in the mother's language. If the father does the same, he will get the word in his language. Many children at this stage will also answer a question like 'What does daddy say?' from the mother with the word in the father's language (which would not usually be used to the mother).

Example

Lisa (2;5) is quite happy with her languages and will say to her mother things like 'Pappa says "macka"' when she gets a sandwich. When asked, 'What does mamma say?' she will say something like 'Mamma says "sam-mich".' On one occasion she was asked, 'What does Lisa say?' and she fell silent, looking totally nonplussed.

The child on this level who has realised that there are two systems used by different people has not really caught on to the notion of her own bilingualism. She sees that her parents each use a different system to her and she to them. Her perception of her parents as monolingual speakers of the language they use to her has not been affected by her having heard her parents use the other language to other people, even to each other.

In families which use the one person–one language way of working, some children take the family's convention of who speaks which language to whom a step further and make it into an unbreakable rule. These children will go out of their way to avoid using a word of the inappropriate language to the 'wrong' parent, and will refuse to answer a question which requires this. They may become upset if spoken to in the 'wrong' language, or may find it very funny, even if they are quite used to hearing the parent speak the language to other people. In fact many children assume that all adults are monolingual and may be either horrified or vastly amused if someone outside the immediate family addresses them in the minority language if they know that person to be a majority language speaker.

Examples

Patrik (3;10) attended a monolingual Swedish pre-school. One day, when he was being picked up to go home another child's father said, 'Bye-bye Pat.' Patrik started sniggering and broke into peals of laughter.

Leif (4;0) wanted to join in his father's 'speaking English' game, but could not bring himself to produce any actual English words when speaking directly to his father. When his dad said, 'Hello Leif, how are you?' Leif wanted to answer, but could not break the iron rule he himself had set up forbidding the inappropriate language to be used, and so answered his father in gibberish.

There were set rules that we spoke English to you and Swedish to Pappa. You knew where to go if you had a question in English, and then with Swedish to Pappa. But it was a bit confused – I mean it looked confused from the outside. From the inside? No, it wasn't very complicated.

(Leif, 23)

Active and passive languages

It is not unusual for children to go through a phase of arguing about what things are called (at about 18 months to three years – the same time as they start arguing about everything else!). A child who insists that a table is a chair can be told that he is wrong, but a child who insists on saying the Spanish *mesa* instead of *table* to her French mother is not really wrong, but just not using the appropriate language. Sometimes children at this age and right on up will prefer a word in one language for some reason and use only that word in both languages, even when they know the word in the other language. Correcting this kind of inappropriate language use can be an uphill struggle, but it may be necessary, especially if words from the majority language are appearing more and more in a child's minority language speech. Accepting the children's use of these words can be the thin end of the wedge, and before you know what has happened the children may be speaking only the majority language. Our policy has been to make sure we use the word in the appropriate language in our response, in case the child did not know it. If that is not enough we would point out that, for example, 'sommarlov in English is summer holidays'. Of course, many families quite systematically and naturally use certain majority language words when there is no adequate way to express what is meant in the minority language. This is usually when discussing things specific to the society of the country in which the family lives.

In many families where the children do not actively speak the minority language even when it is spoken to them the reason may be that one parent is solely responsible for the child's linguistic development in the minority language. If this parent is not able to spend a great deal of time with the child from an early age there may be problems. Many parents, often fathers, in this position find that they need to spend more time at work than is optimal for their children's linguistic development. For the reasons mentioned above, this may not work very well, although even a passive knowledge of the father's language is well worth having, and invaluable in communicating with relatives. This kind of passive competence in a language can relatively easily be switched to an active command of the language given favourable circumstances and sufficient motivation as the child gets older, for example going alone to visit cousins who are monolingual speakers of the child's second (passive) language.

Another set of circumstances which may lead to a passive command of the second language is if the minority language parent uses both the minority and the majority language when addressing the child. This can easily become a habit, particularly if monolingual majority language-speaking children are regularly present in the home. The choice is then between (a) saying everything twice, once in each language, (b) speaking only the minority language and letting the majority language children feel left out, or letting the children who know both languages translate for them, and (c) speaking only the majority language to all the children. This last solution is often adopted, and can lead to the children answering their minority language parent in the majority language, and eventually becoming reluctant to use the minority language at all.

An additional problem here is that if the minority language parent does not use the minority language in front of majority language speakers, perhaps so that they will not feel left out or feel that they are the subject of discussion, the child may come to feel that the minority language is inferior and not fit for use in public. This can lead to the child becoming embarrassed if the parent uses this language in public places. If things go so far that the minority language parent feels obliged to speak his or her second language in public and even in private to the child, the parent may seem diminished in the eyes of the child. Rather than being eloquent speakers, able to argue convincingly for the principles they believe in, immigrant parents can become hesitant, clumsy speakers in the majority language. Bringing up a child, with all that it involves, of singing nursery rhymes and reading aloud, persuading, scolding, coping with teenage rhetoric and tantrums and setting limits, is infinitely more difficult through the medium of a second language than through one's native language. This is also an argument for parents to whom it might not seem quite natural to speak their own, minority, language at all to their child if they have no one else to speak it to. Even the most innocent-looking infant will turn into a teenager in time!

Due to differences in the amount of stimulation and input the child gets in each language, one or other of the child's languages may be dominant at different times. In families where the minority language is spoken to the child by both parents at home, this will be the first dominant language. If the parents each speak their own language to the child, the mother's language may be dominant initially if she spends most time with the child. If the mother's language is the minority language it will probably be overtaken by the majority language when the child starts pre-school or school, if not before. The minority language may again become dominant if an extended stay (of at least a month) in a country where the minority language is spoken can be arranged.

This transfer to majority language speech at the expense of the minority language often seems to come at around two and a half years of age. This happened in several of the families I interviewed. For some it was the end of the child's active use of the minority language, for others a trip to a country where the minority language is spoken was enough to turn things around and get the child talking the minority language again. This was my experience with Leif at this age. After a week in Ireland he returned to answering me in English. Some of the families who told me about their situation feel that things might have been better if they had done something different:

> Perhaps I would not have responded to my children when they spoke to me in Spanish, if I had it to do over again, in order to oblige them to use English. Basically I suppose that they have assimilated English and that their passive knowledge can be made active when they decide that they want to use English, for whatever reason.
>
> (Sean Golden, Barcelona)

> It might have been even better if I had held to some 'rule' of always speaking English to them and not Swedish, but in reality I think that would have been difficult to achieve. I have submitted to the reality that Sweden is their native country, they have Swedish friends, Swedish schools, but have always maintained that I am American, not Swedish. Our family rules are a mixture of both cultures, so that when they visit their American relatives they can feel a part of that culture as well.
>
> (Nancy Holm, Sweden)

> I am disappointed that we could not keep the languages in their life more than we have. All of our close friends are bilingual but different languages. I wish now that my husband and I had made a pact. I studied his language but I am not proficient in Arabic. We even tried to start an Arabic-language school with other Arabic-speaking families but it lasted about three months. I don't really know the answer. If the schools had supported the second language by offering a second language that would have been tremendous. I have my sons signed up for Spanish summer camp. I try. I really want them to be bilingual. Everything could have been better with more support in the community through the school. Also it would have helped if my husband and I spoke the same native language or at least tried to learn it on a deeper level. We both regret not being clearer in our expectations and in which language to commit to.
>
> (Mother in North Carolina)

Interference and mixing

Children who grow up simultaneously learning two (or more) languages usually go through a phase when they mix languages. At the one word utterance level the words seem to come quite indiscriminately from one or other of the languages. By the two or three word stage, mixing is occurring a lot, giving utterances like 'min book' (my book) or 'jag want some' (I want some) from Lisa (2;0 and 2;4), or Patrik (4;0) saying 'gör so here' (from Swedish *gor så här* (do this)). This mixing phase gets more or less sorted out with time, and children usually learn to keep the languages separate. This is not, however, always the way it works. Some older children may substitute majority language words for minority ones in a minority language sentence without turning a hair. When pushed, they may in fact know all the words they need, but just say the first ones that come into their head, regardless of which language they belong to.

> **Example**
>
> I don't want to åka to skolan, how many more veckor is it in the sommarlov? (I don't want to go to school, how many more weeks are there in the summer holidays?)
>
> (Leif, 9;7)

At home, where everyone understands both languages, this kind of hotchpotch serves its purpose: the sentence is understood without difficulty. With monolingual English-speaking relatives, no mixing occurs. It is not that the child cannot keep the languages apart, rather that he does not choose to. While purists may despair, it is positive that he at least ostensibly speaks the minority language, English, at all. Leif (9;7) still stuck to his rule of speaking English to his mother, but had given up making the slight effort to recall the English word when the Swedish word comes to mind first. At seven, he would ask for vocabulary items before embarking on a sentence. As a laid-back nine-year-old, he felt that as long as the communication works it does not matter how. At 12 he would still sometimes produce this kind of mixed sentence, although he was able to repeat the sentence, substituting all the Swedish words with English ones on request. It is more difficult to make him aware of the grammatical interference from Swedish.

Interference between the languages can be much more subtle than this kind of word substitution. Nuances of meaning and false friends may cause no end of misunderstanding, as well as amusement, for children with two languages. Similarly, in their effort to make sense of the linguistic chaos around them, children with two languages may use direct translation between their languages, assuming that a word which has a certain translation in one context will always have that translation.

Examples

The English word hat has a wider meaning than the similar Swedish word *hatt*, which means top hat, bowler or lady's hat, while the Swedish *mössa* covers caps and the kind of woolly hats children wear. Children talking in Swedish about their *hattar* cause no end of amusement.

The Swedish word *nos* refers to the muzzle of an animal. Anders (3;4) would use it instead of the correct *näsa* in exclamations such as 'Min nos!' when he wanted his nose wiped.

The Swedish word for snowman is *snogubbe*; gingerbread man is *pepparkaksgubbe*; the green man when you cross the road is *grön gubbe*; the man in the moon is *gubben i manen*. Leif (3;0) transferred this to all occasions when he wanted to say man in Swedish, always using *gubbe*, which in fact means 'old man' and is not very polite to say about people within their earshot.

Other kinds of interference between the languages can also be observed. Perhaps the most obvious is foreign accent. The majority language spoken outside the family, at school and everywhere else usually becomes older children's dominant language. Very many children brought up with two languages speak the minority language with an accent. This may come as a surprise or even a shock to some parents (it certainly did to us!): were they not supposed to be able to learn to speak without an accent if they started early enough? This seems in part to depend on the child's linguistic ability, so that children who happen not to be fortunate enough to have an ear for languages may end up with the same kind of foreign accent as any majority language speaker would have in the minority language. In the same way as Leif puts Swedish words into an English sentence, he also puts Swedish sounds into English words. Somehow, perhaps because of the relatively small amount of input in English, he has failed to develop a fully separate phonological system and phonotactics for English. This is something we have also observed in other Swedish–English-speaking children in Sweden. Interestingly, the children's foreign accent seems to be diminishing as they grow older and become more aware of the phonetic differences between the languages. This might be an effect of their English lessons in school. They have, for example, learned to pronounce <th> so that Leif (12;0) and Anders (10;3) corrected Patrik (6;5) and Lisa (4;10) when they said <f> instead of <th>.

Examples

Leif (8;5): 'I fink so' and Patrik (4;0): 'Fank you' (even if the pronunciation of <th> as <f> is not unusual even in monolingual English-speaking children, it is not a feature of the speech of anyone they hear).

Leif (5;0): 'Wery good!'

Anders (7;8) pronounced the sound sequences <rn>, <rt>, <rd>, <rs>, <rds>, etc. as retroflex sounds, something like English <n>, <t>, <d>, <sh>, <dsh> with the tongue tip turned upwards and backwards in accordance with Swedish phonology rules, so that 'birds' becomes something like 'birch'. This was still observable on occasion at 15;2, but at 22 it has completely disappeared.

The British English variation between 'light' and 'dark' <l> was long missing from Leif's and Anders' speech, so that they pronounced both the <l> in 'light' and the <l> in 'well' without raising the back of the tongue, but they have developed this distinction as they grew older. Patrik and Lisa have always been able to produce a dark <l>.

The voiced z-sound at the end of words like 'flies' is pronounced as an unvoiced hissing <s>.

Leif (9;5): the Swedish vowels /i:/ and /y:/ are confused so that 'by' (village) became 'bi' (bee) in a school dictation.

Sentence structure can often be affected by transfer from one language to the other, giving howlers such as 'I want not' (Leif, 5;3) for 'I don't want to', which is a word-for-word translation from the Swedish 'Jag vill inte', and conversely 'Jag vill ha ett glas av vatten' ('I want a glass of water' (Anders, 7;5)), where the 'av' should not be in the Swedish sentence. The older boys later became very aware of these kinds of differences (which are explicitly taught in school English lessons) and still correct each other and their younger brother and sister regularly, although they do not speak English together.

When these children began to travel independently they got more exposure to the minority language, English. Their early experience and excellent understanding of the spoken language have stood them in good stead and provided a solid basis on which their vocabulary and grammar have been developed. Even as children, they had an extensive passive vocabulary in English and they were willing and able to communicate with English speakers, and had no difficulty making themselves understood or understanding what was said to them. When they came to learn English at school, they managed well, which they might not have without the early input. The possible effect on Leif's majority (dominant) language Swedish is potentially more serious, but has by no means ever reached the stage where he seems non-native. However, as is clear from the interviews with Patrik, Anders and Leif reported in Chapter 10, they do feel that their Swedish is affected by English to a certain extent.

A feature of all kinds of language learning of this kind, where languages are used only in certain circumstances or to certain people (e.g. English is used only to mother, grandmother and mother's friends and their children, while Swedish is used everywhere else), is that vocabulary in the two languages is learned unevenly. The children may know all sorts of words and phrases in English associated with things they have done with their mother, maybe cooking, gardening, cycling, letter-writing, setting the table or making beds. They may not know the corresponding words in Swedish at all, even if it is their dominant language. By the same token they may never have heard the English words for father-type activities, such as fixing the car, sweeping the floor, playing football or working in the forest.

Children are individuals even if they grow up with two languages. What is true for one child may not be for another. No two children have the same combination of strengths and weaknesses even if they are brought up in the same family. Leif and Anders are a good example of this. Leif's Swedish has been dominant since he started pre-school and his English has not developed to a point where it could be called native-like, although he does have a functional command of English which far exceeds that of his monolingual peers. Anders was at 7;10 about equally strong in both languages. At 10;3 his Swedish was clearly dominant but his English was good, even if his vocabulary was limited by his reluctance to read English books and a lack of English speakers to interact with. His pronunciation was less accented and he hardly ever used Swedish words in English sentences. At 14;10 he was native-like in both languages. He had then much better sentence structure than Leif ever had in English. He simply had a better ear for languages at this stage, and thus is better equipped to become more monolingual-like in both his languages. Although he himself feels that his knowledge of both languages is somewhat patchy (see Chapter 10 for an interview at age 21), he can certainly pass for native in both languages.

Men and women use language differently; it is often the mother in monolingual families who tries to encourage the children to moderate their language and avoid using slang and non-standard expressions, while the father introduces these expressions, perhaps particularly to his sons. If the mother and father speak different languages, they have no opportunity to balance each other's input to the children. The boys' use of their mother's language (English in the case of the children in the

examples) may lack a masculine input, sounding perhaps slightly femi-
nine. Conversely, the girls' Swedish, with no mother's touch to moderate the father's speech, may have a tomboyish tone, such as Lisa (2;5):
'Nu ska vi käka' ('Grub's up!' – literally, 'Now we're going to eat',
where 'käka' is a slang word for 'eat'), which is quite inappropriate from
a two-year-old girl!

> Parents should stress the importance of both languages. At first, we
> assumed that if both us parents talked English at home, the kids
> would pick up acceptable Chinese outside the home. Later we
> realised my son was speaking a variety of Mandarin we found crude
> and unsophisticated. The situation improved greatly when my
> husband began speaking Mandarin with him at home. Input from
> both parents in both languages is needed, in my opinion, for kids to
> pick up the 'elaborated' version of a language.
>
> (Karen Steffen Chung, Taiwan)

The critical period hypothesis

If you learn a single language from infancy, you are said to be a native
speaker of that language. As long as you get sufficient input in another
language, you might be able to achieve native-speaker competence in
that language. Unfortunately, it is difficult to get that much input and
practice in more than one language. There are, perhaps, some fortunate
individuals who can call themselves balanced bilinguals, and who master
two (or more) languages as natives, but it is much more common, even
among those who have learned two languages from infancy, that one
language becomes dominant and the other is less than native-like.

An adult who comes to a new country and learns the language
spoken in that country as an adult will not usually approach native standard. A motivated and/or talented learner may achieve near-native
proficiency in the grammar, vocabulary and semantics of the target
language, but only exceptional learners will ever come to sound native
as well. Small children are able to learn to speak a second language
without any trace of a foreign accent, just as they learned their first
language. The reasons for this are not fully understood. One possible
explanation is encompassed in the critical age or critical period
hypothesis, which states that there is a period in a child's development
when language acquisition occurs with very little effort, and that after a
certain age the brain is no longer able to learn language in this way.
This is based on early theories concerning brain lateralisation and neural

plasticity (Penfield 1965; Lenneberg 1967). There is no general agreement about what age this is, but puberty has been suggested as a likely candidate (Major 1990). The critical period hypothesis is not uncontroversial. It has been suggested that differences between child and adult learning patterns may be due to a number of uncontrollable social and cultural factors (Flege 1987). Thomas Scovel's book *A Time to Speak* (1988) gives an excellent exposition of this topic. Scovel concludes that there is a critical period for pronunciation, but finds no evidence that the critical period hypothesis holds true for other aspects of second language learning. He suggests that there may be sociobiological reasons why accents solidify at puberty. It is at that time that other aspects of the individual's perception of his or her own identity surface, and it is therefore appropriate that individuals are marked as belonging to a particular group just then.

Major (1990) found evidence to suggest that it might not be possible for adults who have acquired only one language during the critical period and who have later been exposed to a second language to acquire or maintain native-like proficiency in pronunciation in both languages. This would mean that if they were to achieve native-like proficiency in a second language, it would be at the price of native proficiency in the first language. Alternative scenarios would be the maintenance of native proficiency in the first language while native-like proficiency in the second language is never achieved (this is the most common situation for second language learners), or loss of native proficiency in the first language while never acquiring it in the second language. This is quite common among immigrants who spend many years away from their native countries. They are regarded as foreigners in the country in which they live, and find that they are also regarded as foreigners, or at least as different, in their country of origin, because they have partially lost or modified their first language. This is a difficult situation in which to find oneself and entirely in line with the feeling of being a foreigner both in the new country and the country of origin:

> Several times, when I was in France some people have told me that I had an American accent when I spoke French. But I can't really believe, nor understand this.
>
> (Stephanie Lysee, USA)

> And expect that, if you become fluent in the L2 [second language], your L1 will suffer, unless you have an unusual circumstance with lots of contact to both languages in a lot of domains. Although we

think of language transfer as being 'bad', it is the most normal thing in the world.

(Janet Fuller, USA)

I think I can speak reasonably good and accent-free Dutch even after having been away for more than forty years, but it comes slowly. When in Holland I cannot hang on to Dutch and I automatically (in the heat of ambient conversational speech) [shift] to English.

(Henry K. van Eyken, Quebec)

I would emphasise that they [immigrants] do not and probably should not sacrifice their L1 in order to acquire (and become fluent) in L2. Although they need to be flexible and open to new culture as well as to language, it's possible to add one new language rather than replace it.

(Aya Matsuda, Indiana)

Chapter 5

The child with two languages

Children who grow up with two languages have a unique chance to acquire them both in a way that is not possible for those who meet their second language later in life. These children have potential access to the riches of two cultures, and may become extraordinarily linguistically and culturally competent adults, with the best of two worlds. These children are especially favoured and privileged. However, the presence of two languages may well give them some trouble at all levels of language learning. Children find themselves in a position where they are exposed to more than one language through no doing of their own. We adults have made the choices: the children have not chosen any part of the experience they are going through. It is, therefore, up to us to make things as easy as possible for them, while helping them to get the maximum benefit from the situation.

Advantages and disadvantages of two languages for the child

For the youngest children, living with two languages is primarily negative. Their initial attempts to analyse the stream of sound flowing over them into meaningful units are hindered by the sheer number of different words they hear. Later they need to learn two words for everything and two systems for putting words together. They also have to understand the system of rules regulating who uses which language to whom and when. Failure to grasp the mechanisms of this system will lead to frustration and failed communication, which must be added to the communication difficulties experienced by any child just beginning to talk.

Example

Our children's Swedish paternal grandmother said of Anders when he was two, 'I can't understand what he is saying, I think it is English.' In fact it was Swedish, but so unclear that only a parent could interpret it.

Older children also have to work harder if they regularly use two languages. They are required to learn more words (although they may not have as large a vocabulary as monolingual speakers even in their dominant language) and more ways of saying things. They will be expected to achieve literacy in both languages, a task which is daunting enough for some children in a single language. However, children learning two languages with alphabetic writing systems will not have to go through all the steps of learning to read twice. The principles of alphabetic writing are common to all the languages of Europe and many other languages. Languages like Greek, Arabic, Thai and Russian have alphabetic systems, and children who can read in one language can usually transfer their acquired decoding skills to another language, even if the correspondences between letters and sounds are not quite the same in both languages. Children needing to learn to read and write Chinese or Japanese as well as a language with an alphabetic writing system have a harder time.

Acquiring literacy in the minority language can open up a new world of literature and thereby language to the child. No amount of visiting the country where the language is spoken or contact with other speakers can give a child as rich a vocabulary and such a mastery of the nuances of the language as a thorough immersion in its children's literature. In some countries, such as Sweden, some municipalities offer education in some home languages (although recent cutbacks have affected this activity severely), often concentrating on reading and writing. In other countries, for example England, Saturday schools run by the local minority language community have served the same purpose. If neither of these options is available, it is up to the parents to support their children as best they can either within the family or in co-operation with other families in a similar situation. (See Appendix A for ideas for a parents' workshop.)

There are many advantages for the child who has a reasonable mastery of a second language. In the case of an immigrant family, where both parents come from the same language background, the child will need the minority language to communicate with the parents, assuming that the parents use the minority language, even if the child answers them in the majority language. The majority language is needed for school and social activities, and there is not usually any problem getting children to use it. In the case of the mixed language family, the minority language may not be essential for communication; the parent who speaks that language may have at least some knowledge of the majority language for his or her own needs. In both these types of families, a child who can speak or at least understand the minority language has a channel open for communication not only with the parent or parents who speak the language, but also with grandparents, cousins and family friends and their children.

Some children find that their abilities in a second language give them a sense of pride. This is probably dependent on whether the minority language and its speakers have high or low prestige among other children. English is a particularly favoured language in many countries: young people in many parts of the world learn English and admire English-speaking musicians and actors. This means that a child for whom English is the minority language may be very motivated to speak it well, because of a kind of admiration from peers.

When children who can use both their languages go to visit the country where the minority language is spoken, their hard work and that of their parents are seen to be worthwhile. At best, the children find that they can communicate with those around them. Children with passive skills in the minority language at home may blossom into active speakers when they find themselves surrounded by monolingual speakers of the language.

If parents have encouraged their children by praising their skills in the minority language, which is, of course, generally a very good thing to do, the children may be devastated to realise that they are not actually indistinguishable from monolingual speakers of the minority language. The possibility also exists that the children are not actually fully aware of the cultural differences between the countries. The children may think they are more bilingual and bicultural than they are. This may not be a problem, and can help a shy child to dare to use the weaker language, so there may be no need to disillusion such children.

Being different

In many countries, talking a language other than the majority language in public places will attract attention. How much attention depends on how accustomed the population is to foreign residents and tourists. Interested strangers may ask questions about the children, whether they are bilingual, where they or the parent come from, and so on. Some may even go so far as to offer unsolicited advice about what the parents are doing wrong. Others may be full of admiration for these children who get a second language 'for free'.

Young children are not usually embarrassed by this kind of interest, although they probably will not want to be the object of attention. At some point children become aware that they have two languages and that this is not usual. Sometimes children in their continuous trial and error striving to make sense of the way of the world will come up with odd theories. My son Anders (3;0) asked if all Mummies speak English, and was quite fascinated by a male visitor from England; he had assumed that men just do not speak English, at least not to children! By the same token, it can be difficult for a parent used to speaking his or her native language to children to switch to the majority language to speak to the children next door.

Some older children may be unwilling to be seen in public with their minority language-speaking parent or parents. They do not want to be made an exhibition of by being spoken to in the minority language; still less would they want to be heard speaking it. In many families, youngsters have lopsided discussions with their immigrant parent where the parent uses the minority language and the child answers in the majority language. At home, they may or may not all speak the minority language. For such children it might be even worse if their parent spoke the majority language in public, especially if his or her command of the language is less than perfect.

Example

An American musician living in Sweden gives occasional concerts. Sometimes his children are in the audience, but they dread him pointing them out to the audience or addressing them directly from the stage because of his strong American accent and poor Swedish.

There was one moment of crisis when my daughter, not long after she started school at the age of four, said to me in Spanish, 'Daddy don't speak to me in English in the street.'

(David, Galicia)

At a certain age many youngsters find a reason to be ashamed of their parents, even if they do not have another language or come from another country. They may be too rich or too poor or too ugly or too famous or have the wrong car or the wrong clothes or whatever! Most children do not want to stick out in the crowd, and believe they would prefer parents who are exactly like everyone else's:

> My family emigrated to the USA when I was a child, and I grew up there, but always conscious of being different from the neighbours' children, who commented on my parents' accents, for instance, or because my parents didn't understand American sports, or care about them, and because my parents' social circle was almost entirely restricted to fellow Irish immigrants, most of whom were Irish speakers from Dingle or Connemara.
>
> (Sean Golden, Barcelona)

> My mother always encouraged the Italian language within the family, and the Italian culture. I was ashamed of it as a teenager. Of the Italian, of the loudness, of the passionate nature.
>
> (Loretta, a Londoner in Sweden)

> I acquired Spanish in my childhood, and I didn't understand that my parents, as adult learners, faced a more difficult task. They were trying to learn a language just by interacting with native speakers, without any formal training or any materials besides a pocket dictionary, but I didn't think of that. I honestly thought there was something wrong with them. Not my father, actually; my perception back then was that he wasn't really trying. He would, for instance, resort to the reasonable strategy of using one or two verb forms in all situations, even when they didn't fit. My mother, on the other hand, seemed to be trying very hard; I couldn't understand how she seemingly 'forgot' how to pronounce a word right after I told her how.
>
> (Mai Kuha, USA)

> Our children used to say that I should not speak Spanish as my accent sounds like a Cuban, and would get embarrassed when I would speak!
>
> (R. Chandler-Burns, Mexico)

Bringing home friends

From pre-school right up until they leave home, most children want to bring home their friends from time to time. Generally, the friends are likely to be majority language speakers. Depending on how the family language system works, this may or may not be a problem. Obviously, everything said to visiting children must be in the majority language unless the minority language happens to be a school language, in which case the visitors (if they are good enough in the school language) might be expected to be able to handle (and benefit from) conversation in the minority language, even if they answer in the majority language:

> Recently, some of our younger son's friends have asked us to deliberately speak English in front of them, so they'll get a feeling for what the language really sounds like (as opposed to their English teachers' non-use of the language). No problem. Interesting, though. It would be nice to know if these kids' attitude towards bilingualism changed because of this experience; we never will.
>
> (Harold Ormsby L., Mexico)

> Last weekend my son came home with his girlfriend and we were sitting at the table and it was bilingual still even though she was sitting there. English is a language that she'll understand well, so we didn't feel we were alienating her in any way. Eventually, I was speaking to her in English too and she was answering me in English so it was all very familiar for everyone.
>
> (Loretta, Sweden)

If the family system involves speaking the minority language exclusively to the children, perhaps everything can be translated for the benefit of the visitor, or, especially for older children, an exception can be made and everyone can go over to the majority language while the visitor is there. The same applies with an adult visitor, except that an adult visitor might not feel the same pressing need to know exactly what is being said to the children. There is a risk that sensitive visitors might feel left out of minority language conversations, or even that remarks about them are being made in the minority language.

Some children might not have prepared their friends for the linguistic scene at home. It could be difficult for them to explain to classmates that they are not the monolinguals they appear to be. Children who grow up with two languages probably take it for granted and may not realise that others may find the situation odd or difficult. While they may not try to keep their bilingual background a secret, they might not actually talk about it:

> At nursery school he is very popular. Mothers of other children try to get Peter to make friends with their child, probably in hopes that

their child will get early experience with English and foreign culture.

(John Moore, Japan)

Day-care and school

For children who use only the minority language at home, the first extended encounter with the majority language comes when they start to play with neighbouring children or when they go to day-care or pre-school. Provided that they get enough contact with native speakers of the majority language at pre-school, their acquisition of the majority language is usually rapid. They are of course extraordinarily motivated to find a channel for communication. Problems may arise if minority language-speaking children rarely meet native speakers of the majority language, as may happen in areas with large immigrant populations.

Older children who move with their families to a new country may have greater problems. This is especially true if they have already started school. They may lose a year or more of schooling before their majority language skills are good enough to let them follow the curriculum work. By that time, they may have fallen behind children their own age. Younger children seem to have fewer problems:

> Before my first son went to the USA, he was fluent in French and he could understand everything in English but would never produce any utterance more than one or two words in English. After his first month in the USA, in kindergarten, he spoke perfectly.
>
> (Gregory Grefenstette, France)

> When I left my daughter in the classroom that first day she whispered, 'Mommy, why are they all speaking Spanish?' – we had come from California – and I whispered back as I rushed out the doors, 'It's French.' So that's how much French she knew. ... By spring she was 'fluent'.
>
> (Peggy Orchowski, USA)

For younger children, who are away from home for the first time at day-care or pre-school, parents may notice that the children lack words in the home language to tell about their day's activities. There are often many gaps in these children's vocabulary, not only in the home language, but also in the majority language. If both parents speak the minority language at home, the child may not know words for events and things at home in the school language. In some municipalities in Sweden and elsewhere pre-school children are offered home language training (if large enough groups can be arranged) for the specific purpose of helping the children to do pre-school things in the minority language, to give them the vocabulary and structures to let them talk about pre-school in the home language. Some parents feel that they need to make sure that their children have some basic knowledge of the majority language before starting school or pre-school, while others are confident that this will be a temporary problem only and that the child will quickly catch up:

> I started thinking about my wife's experiences as an assistant in a kindergarten. She says that the kids that are the most 'uncomfortable' starting in kindergarten are the kids who have only been exposed to a minority language, and no Norwegian. This, of course (like everything else), varies a lot from child to child, but children who are already in a difficult situation aren't exactly helped by the fact that they don't understand a word that is said by either the adults or the other kids. To me, this is obvious, but many parents seem to be very eager to get their children to talk the minority language as early as possible, without regard to the fact that the language that the child will be using on a daily basis is neglected. After all, to most people, the mother tongue is the most important, so also for children. My opinion is that the language the child will be using on a daily basis with other people should be the most important to start with. Of course, as soon as the child is 'up and running' on the main language, or gets 'other help' (teachers, other children) with the majority, the focus could very well be switched to the minority language ... and most important: don't let your expectations of having a bilingual child make life more difficult than necessary for your children (note the 'more than necessary').
>
> (Roar Pettersen, Norway)

> As Isis has developed interests separate from her activities with her mother, she has learned a lot of English vocabulary for which she lacks the Portuguese equivalents. This makes it very hard for Isis to express herself in Portuguese sometimes, and she tends to give up on saying something to her mother if she lacks more than a single word for whatever she's trying to talk about. For this reason, my wife has tried to read more Portuguese bedtime stories to her, just as a way of exposing her to more words that she needs to know.
>
> (Don Davis, Boston)

If the minority language is a school language

If your child's second language is a compulsory school language there are many things to think about. In the case of English in Sweden (and in many other countries) children start to learn English in first, second or third grade (aged seven to nine). Initially they learn only words. Gradually the amount of English teaching each week is increased, until, by the age of 16, they are supposed to have a fair command of written and spoken English. Children who speak English at home with one or both parents will naturally get very little out of this teaching. The first vocabulary learning and sentence construction exercises will be far too easy. The teacher is then faced with the problem of pupils who (a) are bored, (b) know all the answers and (c) either want to show off their knowledge or cringe in embarrassment if the teacher draws attention to their situation. The teacher may at that point appoint the children as assistant teachers, or give them work of their own to do, which is infinitely preferable. The problem is that children who have been living and breathing English all their lives desperately need help with the language, just as monolingual children do with their first language, but they require mother tongue education, not foreign language teaching. A sensitive teacher might be able to arrange suitable work for such a child if proper home language teaching by a native speaker is not available or if the child needs to stay in the foreign language classroom.

Since most school teachers are native speakers of the majority language, their skills in the foreign language are unlikely to be perfect. What is a child who is a speaker of the language being taught to do if he feels the teacher to be wrong about some point of the language she is teaching? If the child corrects the teacher, the teacher will be embarrassed. The child may not even be correct: his mastery of the target language is probably far from perfect. If the teacher corrects the child, he may be affronted in his capacity as a kind of native speaker. The child's minority language is often modelled on a single speaker, the parent, who may speak a different dialect from the standard dialect learned as a foreign language by the teacher. Most importantly, children's time should not be wasted by obliging them to sit through instruction which is patently unsuitable for them. Children with two languages have special needs if they are to reach their full potential in both their languages.

My own experience of having children learning English at school with their monolingual classmates is mixed. The teaching has been useful in pointing out differences between English and Swedish sentence structure. One problem has been pronunciation. Many of the teachers and education students I have encountered in schools and at Swedish universities (where many take the obligatory English component in teacher training) have strong Swedish accents. Naturally they pass their Swedish accent on to their pupils – the younger the pupils, the closer the approximation to the teacher's pronunciation. When I pointed out a mispronunciation to one of our children, his reaction was that he preferred to pronounce the word like the teacher.

Another problem has been that a child may feel they know better than the teacher but in fact the teacher is right. I have had discussions with one of my children's teachers asking me to point out to the child that the teacher may be right sometimes, and even having me go through a point of grammar in the book with the child, to convince him that I agree with the teacher on this one.

> They [my children] speak Spanish with a Catalan accent. They have no accent in Catalan. They speak English with a Spanish/ Catalan accent at times, other times without. They study English in school, since their third year of primary school, which is worse, because they adapt themselves to the pronunciation and grammar of the teacher and/or their fellow students, who are in every case non-native. They don't want to be conspicuous or act as native informants, although everyone expects them to be fluent in English.
>
> (Sean Golden, Barcelona)

> My son keeps a low profile in English class. His spoken English is much better than the teacher's, but he has learned grammar and spelling at school. In general he seems bored in English class, and gets annoyed at mistakes in the texts and tests, but since he has such a heavy class load, and must now prepare for a difficult senior high school entrance exam, he is glad to have an easy subject.
>
> (Karen Steffen Chung, Taiwan)

> Knowing Spanish came in handy during my junior high and high school days when I elected to enrol in Spanish classes so that I could get an 'easy' A.
>
> (Anonymous, USA)

> Have a discussion with the teacher and tell her about your home life, the level of English proficiency, and find the right level of English training so that the kids don't get bored with the class.
>
> (Nancy Holm, Sweden)

I speak German fluently (although apparently with an English intonation pattern), but my written German is less advanced. I took a couple of German courses in university, but because I learned German as a spoken language, rather than 'academically', I found it difficult to understand the grammatical methods used to explain the concepts which I was having difficulty with.

(Michele Disser, Canada)

Literacy

In some schools in some countries, home language education is offered to children with two languages. In most places no such provision is made, and it is up to the local minority language community (if there is such a thing) or the parents if the children are to become biliterate. Many parents wonder if they should try to teach their children to read in the minority language before they start school, where they will learn to read in the majority language. Unless the parent is knowledgeable about reading techniques, or is willing to study methods for teaching children to read, it will be easier to wait until the child can read in the majority language before going to the weaker language. As we have seen, children whose two languages use alphabetic writing systems can apply the principles of decoding writing that they learn for one language to the other language.

However, children are individuals, and some children just cannot wait to start reading. If you feel you would like to try, then the minority language is probably a good place to start. I have tried showing flashcards to all my two- to three-year-olds, with mixed results. Leif learned to recognise about 30 words, but did not really enjoy the exercise. He is still not a keen reader in either language. Anders was completely uninterested, but learned to read by himself, first Swedish then English when he was five (school starts at age seven in Sweden). At seven he began to read Swedish for pleasure and at about 10;10 he discovered Harry Potter, which started him off reading in English. Patrik loved the flashcard method and could read simple English and Swedish texts fluently before he was four. I stopped teaching him at all when he knew 200 words by sight and he worked out phonics in both languages from there by himself. Lisa was not at all interested in flashcards, but by 4;10 she was able to read simple words in both languages. By 9;5 she enjoyed reading in both languages. The point I want to make is that all children are different. Learning to read a second language is not all that difficult if a child can already read one (provided both languages use alphabetic scripts). Let the children lead the way: you will know when they are ready.

Many children are not ready to learn to read until they start school. The school setting provides an important motivation for learning. Some parents find it difficult to set up any kind of structured learning situation at home. If children cannot read or are reluctant readers, read to them! Reading or being read to is an extremely efficient way to increase a child's vocabulary and familiarity with the written language. A side-effect is the widening of experience offered in books, including a good deal of information about the culture in which the book is set. Parents wishing to teach a child about their minority culture will find con-temporary works of fiction set in the country in question very useful. In addition, most children and parents greatly enjoy the shared intimacy of the reading situation.

It might be helpful to structure time for working with each language. Schoolchildren probably have homework, which presumably involves the majority language. Many children want a parent to be with them and take them through their homework. This is particularly valuable for children who do not understand all the teacher's explana-tions. Either parent can help the children, whatever suits the family best. For many children, particularly those who are not keen on doing their homework at all, a regular homework time can be useful, for example after children's TV, before bed. By the same token, some families may find it helpful to reserve some time each week for working with the minority language, that is, reading and writing and doing the kind of work that monolingual children do in their native language. Home schooling or ordinary school materials are probably available from the country the immigrant parent comes from, or can perhaps be obtained through other sources. Ask your relatives or any teacher you know in the appropriate country. You may also be able to order books through a large local bookshop or via the Internet (see the companion website).

Bilingual and minority language schooling

In some places it might be possible to place children in classes which are taught partly or entirely in the minority language. In many parts of the world there are international classes or schools which teach through English, or other languages. There may also be bilingual classes or schools where teaching is both in the local majority language and in English or another language. I have experience of both these school forms in Uppsala, Sweden. International classes for K-9 and bilingual

Swedish/English classes for K–6 are run at an ordinary municipal school in Uppsala.

Anders was in a Swedish class until grade 5 (aged 12). Then he started at the international class in Uppsala along with children from all over the world, many of whom were only in Sweden for a short period and spoke little Swedish. All teaching in this class is in English, with native English speakers as teachers. He stayed in this class until year 9, when he moved to a three-year International Baccalaureate (IB) class for a pre-IB year and the two-year IB programme, which is taught in English in Sweden.

When Lisa was due to start in the first year of compulsory school at the age of seven, a bilingual Swedish–English class was started at the same school. In this class there was one Swedish-speaking teacher and one English-speaking teacher, both natives of the language they were teaching in. After-school care was organised in co-operation with the international classes, i.e. in English. She stayed in that setting until year 4 (when we left Uppsala) and did very well there. While we would not have considered placing either of them in the international class from an early age, because we feel that would have affected their acquisition of Swedish negatively, the bilingual class was a good alternative. Since we planned to live in Sweden for the foreseeable future, it was very important that the children did actually become advanced users of Swedish, and that is difficult without schooling in Swedish.

Chapter 6

Practical parenting in a bilingual home

Help your child to make the most of the situation

If your child is required to live with two languages, there is a lot you can do to help. Even monolingual children do much better if they get support in their linguistic development at home, for example from parents who read to them when they are small and with them when they are older. Children with two languages have more to learn than monolingual children and are therefore in even greater need of support from their parents. Parents in bilingual families need to be very active and to spend a lot of time talking with their children. Books are an important resource. In the mixed language family, the natural thing would be to have each parent read to and sing and play with their child in their own language. Unfortunately, things do not always go as planned. In many monolingual families, only one of the parents, often the mother, ever reads to the children. In spite of the importance of input in both languages, the same may happen in bilingual families. Some parents are, for a wide range of reasons, reluctant to read to their children. If the language spoken by such a parent is the majority language, this is not too big a problem. If the child goes to pre-school, the teachers usually read a great deal to the children, and can to some extent give the child the input they would otherwise have got from a majority language parent. If parents who are reluctant to read are responsible for the minority language, their input is harder to replace. In fact it seems, in our experience, that mixed language families are often more successful at giving their children two active languages if the mother speaks the minority language than if the father does. This will hopefully change as mothers and fathers are increasingly able and willing to share childcare responsibilities.

Home language education and Saturday schools

In some countries, some schools and pre-schools offer special teachers several hours a week for groups of immigrant children or those who have a language other than the majority language at home. In other countries the immigrant communities may organise a Saturday school where a native teacher helps the children with the minority language. This kind of teaching is often aimed at establishing or improving literacy in the minority language. Unfortunately, it is not available to all children. Many children are completely without any kind of support in the community for their minority language. In this case it is up to the parents to help their children and to nurture their linguistic development as well as they are able. Appendix B contains suggestions for supporting a child's minority language with others in play-groups and Saturday schools.

> My children were never offered English as a second language in schools, and even if they were, I doubt if I would have let them attend. It might be different if they were from Iran, but American English is all around them anyway, it has always been a status for them at school and among friends to be American (they are both American and Swedish citizens) and they have never felt 'outside'.
>
> (Nancy Holm, Sweden)

Use any available resources

Parents need to be creative if they are to help their children to become competent speakers of the minority language. They have to arrange for their children to meet other children and adults who speak the minority language so the children understand that there are others who also use the minority language, that it is not a peculiarity only of the child's family. It is particularly valuable for the child to meet other children who speak the minority language so that the child does not only hear adult language. A child who talks only to adults in the minority language may sound precocious and will miss a large part of the language. Of course, the ideal is for children to regularly meet monolingual speakers of the minority language, so that there is no chance of them slipping into the majority language, and so that they will hear speakers who are free from any trace of interference from the majority language:

> I do like to have my children meet other English speakers (both children and adults). I feel that this helps them to understand that speaking English isn't something that only Mommy does.
>
> (Bari Nirenberg, Israel)

One way to arrange this is to make regular trips with the child to countries where the minority language is spoken. This has many advantages for the child's linguistic and cultural awareness, and will give the child a wider experience of the minority language than any other single strategy. Another way is to have monolingual minority speakers visit the family. Suitable visitors might be grandparents, cousins, friends of the minority language parent (especially if they bring their own children), au pairs or exchange students.

When other people are not available for the child to speak to, books, DVDs and satellite or web TV can be helpful. If the child becomes interested in a particular children's TV programme while visiting the minority language country, it may be possible to buy DVDs or books with the same characters. Some children will watch children's programmes over and over again, so that they really come to understand every word that is said, even if they might miss things the first few times. Sometimes children memorise chunks of dialogue from the programmes: so much the better! They will learn a lot about the language that monolingual children their age use. Some families may want to introduce a minority language only policy when they buy DVDs. Some children go through a stage when they want to watch a lot of TV. Parents may feel more comfortable letting small children watch a DVD than TV, so they know what the child is likely to see. If they are going to spend all that time in front of the TV, then let it be in the minority language!

Networking

There are many advantages to getting to know other families who share your linguistic situation. The children benefit from meeting other children who also speak the minority language, and the parents may find they have a lot in common to talk about. In a large city it may not be all that easy to get to know any other residents who may also have the minority language as their native language. The ex-pats in the old days often congregated round the local consulate, but that is not the way things work any more. There may be hundreds of fellow speakers of a language walking around a city, oblivious to one another. Sometimes there may be clubs and societies or informal gatherings which represent different groups, but they do not always broadcast their existence. The local university or college of further education can be a source of information; some foreign language departments are involved in the organisation of, say, local Anglo-Swedish or Greco-Italian friendship associations or language clubs, which may have talks from invited speakers, reading circles, etc. There maybe a language centre nearby which involves native and non-native speakers in joint activities. The British Council (English), Goethe Institut (German), Confucius Institute (Chinese) and Instituto Cervantes (Spanish) have offices in many cities and, like the cultural sections of consulates, they will generally have cultural activities for native speakers and others.

More informal gatherings can be more difficult to locate. English-speaking women, for example, often form such groups in cities across Europe. These are sometimes organised under a larger body, for example American Citizens Abroad, but not always. In several places I am familiar with there are such groups, with English-speaking women from all over the English-speaking world, who meet about every six weeks for a pot-luck supper in one or other of the members' homes or go to a restaurant. These groups offer an invaluable source of contacts for new arrivals, if they are fortunate enough to come across someone willing to tell them about them and to invite them to come along to a party, since membership is by invitation only. This kind of group exists in many places, and could be organised by enterprising individuals in many more places:

> The ESW [English-Speaking Women] is located in Helsinki but has members all over Finland. We do have a newsletter. The organisation was very important to me when I first came to Finland, because 20 years ago almost no one in Finland spoke English; the major foreign language was German. Today most of the newly arrived women don't join us because almost everyone under 30 now speaks fairly good English, especially those who are in/went to university. There is another group, International Women's Club, for all foreign women who live in Finland, but it meets during the morning and is primarily for wives who have accompanied husbands who have temp jobs (two-year tours). There is also an American Women's Club, but it also meets during the day and seems to consist primarily of embassy wives and American businessmen's wives. I was very active in the ESW when I was working at home and raising the kids, because it was my only contact with English and practically my only contact outside the walls of home.
> (Deborah D. Kela Ruuskanen, Finland)

You may be able to meet fellow native speakers through your religious meeting place or through a local adult education organisation. You might be prepared to advertise in the local newspaper, suggesting that fellow countrymen and women contact you, or maybe meet in a pub one evening. You might be surprised at the response! Once you meet others you may be able to arrange activities for the children, such as Saturday school, toddlers' group, play-school or just occasional outings or picnics. Practical suggestions for organising this kind of activity will be found in Appendix B. The following section summarises what I feel to be the most important ways you can help your child.

Practical advice for parents whose child has two languages

- Speak your own language to your child unless there are compelling reasons why another arrangement is preferable.
- Be consistent in your choice of language to a young child. If you want to use different languages with your child in different situations, stick to the system you devise.
- Travel as often as possible to a country where the minority language is spoken. Ideally you should go to the place where the parent responsible for that language is from, especially if there are relatives there for the child to get to know. It is important for these children to realise that their immigrant parent also has a background.
- Meet other children and adults who speak the minority language. Ideally these should be monolingual speakers, since otherwise they might mix the languages or switch to the majority language. Structured activities with other children through the medium of the minority language can be very valuable. For children up to three or four, a parents' and toddlers' group can be a lot of fun for both children and adults. For older children, a play-school with a native minority language-speaking teacher can bring the child's level of language up considerably.
- Try to get hold of and use as many age-appropriate language materials as possible in the minority language: story books and workbooks, tapes, videos, computer games, whatever you and your children feel comfortable with. In a mixed family, both parents should read, talk and play with the children, each in their own language. A child with two languages needs to work and play more with language than a monolingual child who has two parents giving input in a single language. It is just as important to nurture the majority language, which will presumably be the child's dominant language and the language of schooling eventually. Do not leave the majority language to look after itself. Try to support your child's development in both languages just as you would if each was the only language in the family.

- Try to ensure that your child learns to read, and preferably also to write, in the minority language. My experience is that this can be done before or after the child starts school in the majority language, depending on the child's readiness and interest.
- For the sake of the child's weaker language, consider an extended stay in a country where it is spoken as the majority language.
- Consider letting teenagers visit the minority language country on their own, to visit cousins or friends or on a summer exchange visit, or to spend a term or a year in school.
- If the family regularly returns to the same place in a country where the minority language is spoken, for example to visit grandparents, cousins or friends, it may be possible to arrange for even quite young children to attend school for a few days or longer. The potential advantages of this are manifold: the children get to know mono-lingual speakers of their own age, they learn to use their weaker language in different situations, they learn about the culture of the country and they are able to compare their own school with something else, giving them a new perspective on their lives at home.

In my family, we have had mixed results with this kind of mini–immersion in the immigrant parent's language and culture, which two of our children tried in consecutive years in a primary school in Northern Ireland. The first year, both children (aged seven and five at the time) enjoyed their two days in school enormously, revelling in being the centre of attention, each surrounded by a crowd of eagerly curious classmates at each break. They were even invited home to tea on the second day: what an experience that was! The next year, the younger child managed well, but the older child came home in floods of tears at the first break. The teacher had been cross, he said. Not actually at him, but the tone was too far removed from the traditionally calm and encouraging tone in Swedish classrooms. And yes, it has to be said, some of the teachers we saw at the school did seem to try to get order by yelling and snapping at the children. The actual level of discipline does not, however, seem to be any different in the two countries. Well, at least he appreciated his own teacher in Sweden more after that!

We have also sent our older children to stay on their own with relatives and friends in England. While they enjoyed themselves enor-mously, this was much more a cultural experience than a linguistic one. The same is true of having cousins and other English speakers visit us. The children's English is now so well established that this kind of input does little for it, but it is valuable for their sense of background and

belonging to meet as many relatives and other English speakers as possible. With younger children, the situation is quite different and any
minority language-speaking visitor or time spent in an environment
where the minority language is spoken will be immensely valuable for
the child's perception of the language:

> In addition to frequent trips home to Minnesota, I read to them
> most nights, and try to cover things like Greek and Roman myths,
> Mother Goose, the Bible, science books – things I think that can
> give them solid, useful background in English and Western culture.
> (Karen Steffen Chung, Taiwan)

> Consistency, from the first day on, is important. We spoke in
> German, read in German, and had the children listen to a German
> cassette every evening before going to bed.
> (Thomas Beyer, USA)

> I try to spend some time each night going through some short
> reading and writing exercises in German with my kids. They like
> the attention and are therefore rather motivated to learn German
> even when they are tired.
> (Andreas Schramm, Minnesota)

> We really want our daughter to be a bilingual and we are planning
> to have regular play-group sessions with other Japanese-speaking
> children.
> (Kaori Matsuda, Australia)

> One thing I am thinking of and many other Japanese mothers have
> done is to send the child(ren) to their grandparents'/auntie's places
> in Japan during the school holidays. This is very costly but seems to
> be the most effective way. If she can I want her to go to Japanese
> school (primary or secondary) for one year.
> (Kaori Matsuda, Australia)

> In my first years in New York I was sent to a Russian Orthodox
> nursery school where we spoke only Russian. My mother spoke
> Russian and some German to me at home, while my father spoke
> only English (he does not speak or understand any foreign lan-
> guages). When I was seven my parents moved to Washington, DC
> and there was no Russian school, so I started in the US public
> school system. At this time my mother was in close contact with

her brother and sister, both of whom usually speak German with her, so we often switched from Russian to German. I was sent to Germany for three months each summer to stay with relatives and my mother concentrated on speaking mostly German with me at home in order to prepare me for those summers. We also practised reading and writing (my mother is a teacher).

(Ingrid K. Bowman, Hong Kong)

We have a lot of educational videos. We work with pre-school activities in both languages, alternating nights.

(American mother in Sweden)

Because she's home-schooled, she studies her languages formally, a little bit each day. Her favourite is Latin, because her Portuguese makes it easy. ... Chinese is harder, so she doesn't usually like studying it as much, though she likes using it. ... I think a very important factor is praise: people tend, more than they should, to take it for granted that Brazilian kids speak Portuguese, and that Chinese kids speak Chinese. Try to remember that being a polyglot is a difficult achievement, and praise the kid accordingly and constantly for his or her efforts.

(Don Davis, Boston)

Things to do at home

All the above tips show that parents can do a great deal to support all aspects of their child's development. If they are actively involved in what their children are doing they have a better chance of stimulating their development in both their languages. Parents whose children are to acquire two languages do not need to behave any differently from any other parents. The point is that their children are in greater need of active, aware parents who can help them make the most of their languages.

Talk to your child

This may seem obvious, but some parents find they do not actually say all that much to their child, particularly in the first two years before the child has begun to use words to communicate. While small children are extremely good at letting us know what they want even without the use of words, there is no reason for the parent to rely on smiles, gestures and hugs for communication. A chatty parent will be a major resource for the child, letting the child hear a large number of words in many different contexts. A child growing up with two languages has that much more to learn, and needs as much linguistic stimulation as possible in both languages.

Talk to your children about what you are doing, be it changing a nappy or digging the garden. Talk to them about what you will do together later and about what happened yesterday, whether they understand or not. Let the words flow over them. If you talk as though they understand, they will come to understand, and in the meantime they will love the sound of your voice and being with you and having your attention.

If your child is to learn one language from each parent, it may be necessary to ensure that both parents get time to spend with the child. There is often a problem if the parent who is solely responsible for the minority language is not often at home. In many families the father works while the mother is at home with the children, at least while they are small. Even if both parents work, the father may work longer hours than the mother, and may simply not be able to spend enough time with the child. The family may want to take steps to allow the father more time with the children if it is important for them that the children acquire the father's language.

Listen to your child

Communication, even with a tiny baby, is a two-way affair. Given the chance, babies are fully able to take their turn in the conversation, although they may have no words. When you chat to your children, it is important to give them a chance to respond. Ask them questions, and wait for the answer. If you say something like 'Are you hungry then?' to your baby, you will probably get a smile or gurgle in reply. Then you can paraphrase that and expand on it, saying something like 'Yes you are. You're starving, aren't you?' With slightly older children who are starting to talk, you can do the same. Wait for their answer and expand on it or fix it up into a grammatically correct utterance and give it back to them:

PARENT: 'Shall we go shopping?'
CHILD: 'Trolley!'
PARENT: 'Yes, you can sit in the trolley, can't you? You like that, don't you?'

The child who is learning two languages needs exactly the same kind of help as the child who is learning only one language, but more of it.

In addition, the child may need some help to get the languages sorted out, so that if the child in the above example had said the Swedish word 'Vagn!' instead of 'Trolley!', the parent's answer could have been just the same, although this would also be letting the child know that the appropriate word was *trolley*. This can be done without any kind of overt correction, just as part of the conversation. Even older children's errors in one or other of their languages or the use of the 'wrong' language can be dealt with in this same way, by giving the correct form, expanding on what the child said and inviting the child to go on with the conversation.

Keep track of your children's development

David Crystal's excellent book *Listen to Your Child* (1986) has a lot of helpful information for parents who are interested in following the development of their children's language. He suggests that parents track their child's progress by keeping a diary and even making sound recordings. This is not always easy to do, despite the best intentions. Countless professional linguists who start out to document the linguistic development of their own children never actually get very far. Nonetheless, some kind of documentation is interesting and useful to have, especially if you have more than one child, so that you can consult your notes on an older child and see what he or she was saying at the same age as a younger child. The added feature of having two developing languages makes the whole process even more fascinating and provides entertaining reading for children and parents alike in years to come. If you want to record your child, the following points are worth bearing in mind:

- A simple sound recording will do fine unless you think you are likely to want to get involved with advanced editing. Many mobile telephones and audio players have a recording facility. Otherwise you can record directly into a computer using a built-in or external microphone. Free audio programs such as Audacity will let you edit recordings if you want to. Most children are used to seeing computers and mobile devices and will not pay them much attention. One problem with a separate microphone, though, is that small children are often more interested in trying to grab it than in talking.
- Many families have video cameras. The advantages of making a video recording are many. Children may be used to being filmed. Having pictures means that you can document much more about what is going on around the child. It is easier to put the

recording in its context if there are pictures as well as sound, and you can see the child's behaviour as well as hearing speech. Many video cameras have a system for the simple editing of recordings, meaning that a shorter, more interesting film can be made.

- Choose your setting with some care. Ideally, for both sound and video recording, you want to be able to set up the equipment and leave it to look after itself until the recording session is over. We have successfully rigged up the video camera on a high shelf pointing at the kitchen table and recorded whole family mealtimes, from the stressful hungry settling down to the calm sated leaving the table. This can be a good way to make language recordings too. If you want to record one child talking to a parent, try to get any other people out of the room. Provide something for the conversation to be based on: a book, some toys, Play-Doh or whatever you think might work for your child.

- In a mixed language family you will want to record both parents separately interacting with the child, each in their own language. If both parents speak the minority language at home, you may have to invite someone the child knows to come and talk to the child in the majority language, or take the equipment along on a visit to such a person. You may want to make the settings as similar as possible in both languages, and have, say, the child playing with the same toys with both parents in turn, each in their own language.

- On other occasions you might want to document the child's use of language with a brother or sister or visiting friends, or even show how the whole family's interaction is, with frequent language switching and mixing. Then the use of a video camera which is rigged up to film, say, the area round a table can be a great way to get really spontaneous speech. If you are not a part of the conversation you want to record, you will need to provide something for the children to do which will keep them at the table for a while, preferably something that is not too noisy. They will soon forget about the camera, particularly if you leave the room and let them get on with it.

- It is helpful to have a regular time and place to make recordings, so that they are less likely to be forgotten. The first weekend in each month might be about right while children's language is developing rapidly. You do not need to record for very long each time.

- You might like to keep a written record of your child's development. The companion website has pages that can be copied and used to make notes about your child's progress. If you make notes every six months, then you are likely to see considerable development each time.

Read to your child

There is no doubt that regularly reading to young children is a superb way to stimulate their language. Research by Weizman and Snow (2001) showed that parents' use of sophisticated words while reading to their children had a positive effect on the children's vocabulary development. Another study (Isbell *et al.* 2004) found that both reading stories and storytelling are beneficial to children's spoken language development.

Teachers of young children claim to be able to tell which children in their class are read to at home. For a child with two languages, being read to becomes even more important. If children have a limited vocabulary, it is easy for parents to use only words they know their children understand when talking to them, meaning that the children do not often get a chance to learn a new word. Reading books to children opens new worlds to them. If there are many unfamiliar words in the text, you may want to replace some of them with words the children know, but an alternative is to use the word and explain it straight away. Try to follow up the reading in some way; maybe you can use the new words in speaking to the children, asking if they remember what the word was. Children with two languages may need books intended for somewhat younger children in their weaker language:

> I read stories to them in English, at bedtime, and this has shown how limited their vocabulary is. That is, I have almost unconsciously limited the lexicon I use with them, and when I read a children's book to them there are many words, grammatical structures and cultural references they do not understand. ... When I read to them in English now, I make more of an effort to stick to the authentic English vocabulary and syntax, though this means they will miss many details. Sometimes they ask for explanations. More often I slip them in while reading to them.
>
> (Sean Golden, Barcelona)

In a mixed language family who use the one person–one language method with their children, the minority language needs more support than the majority language. The child will be read to in the majority language at school. Nonetheless, being read to is important for both languages. A reasonable compromise might be that the majority parent reads the bedtime story at the weekend and the minority language parent on weeknights. Of course, this will not work in all families, but it might be worth aiming at. Do not stop reading to your children just because they have learned to read. It may be a long time before their reading is fluent enough to let them concentrate on the story rather than on the reading. You can read them stories that will stretch their language, but that would be too difficult for them to read themselves. One of my children found audiobooks in English very useful before her reading skills in English were up to reading the level of book she was ready for intellectually.

Teach your child to read in the minority language

A child who can read is in a position to go on alone into the world of children's literature. Most parents want their children to be literate in both their languages. If home language education is not offered at school or the minority language is not a school subject, you as a parent will have to help. Even if there is help available from school, parents need to ask themselves which language they want their children to read first. In the case of two writing systems which use the same alphabet, there is not much difficulty in learning to read the second language. If the alphabets are different (for example English, Arabic, Greek, Russian) or a totally different writing system is involved (for example Chinese, Japanese) there are more problems.

If you want to teach your children to read the minority language at home before they start school, there are two books to help you get going. Glenn and Janet Doman's *How to Teach Your Baby to Read* (2005) uses flashcards to teach children to sight-read initially, after which they are ready to work out the correspondence between sound and letters on their own. While Doman and Doman recommend their method for young babies, we found an earlier version of this method to work well for one of our children from around two years; our other children were not interested. This kind of reading may not have much value until the children are old enough to understand the words they are reading, but it is a lovely game to play if the child is interested. There are a number of other books on the market on the topic of parents teaching children to read. Whether or not your child actually learns to read before starting school, just the contact and communication between you and your child which the attempt to learn to read involves make it worthwhile.

If you decide to wait with helping your children to read in the minority language until after they have learned to read the majority language, the process may be easier for many children. Having mastered reading in one language, they will often be able to pick it up very quickly in the other language, often without much in the way of formal teaching, just by following the text when they are being read to. The problem then may be to motivate them to read in the minority language when they find it easier in the majority language.

In my experience, children may be reluctant to read in the minority language even after they are technically able to do so. They may find that they are not able to read books at their age level, and that the books they can read are not of interest to them. My solution has been to let the children listen to an audiobook reading of the book while they follow the text in the printed book. This has been successful, although the audiobooks are not always easy to obtain. You may need to find some way to motivate children to read in the minority language, such as some kind of reward system. I found that time on the Internet was a strong motivator for my oldest children at about 10–12 years of age, with 15 minutes' reading (or reading/listening) giving the right to 15 minutes' Internet time. Other children will, of course, find other rewards worth reading for. With all four of my children I have had summer holiday reading schemes, where pages count for points and the target (they pool points for this) has been excursions to an activity park or the like, with various minor rewards along the way.

The point of all this pushing and persuasion is of course to get the children to read enough to discover that reading has its own rewards. When a child becomes an independent reader there is no limit to the amount of vocabulary and language that will be acquired. Extensive reading for pleasure is one of the most efficient ways to develop language both for native and non-native speakers of any age.

Obtain material in the minority language

Other media are also valuable for children. At a certain age, many children want to do nothing but watch their favourite films or DVD series over and over again. You might like to enforce a minority language only policy for DVDs. Even if TV-watching is generally of limited value, a four-year-old who watches the best modern children's programmes for the umpteenth time is learning his minority language in a way he never could if he saw the programme only once; he is learning a lot about the culture of the country in which the programme is set, he is getting the same kind of children's culture as his peers in the minority language-speaking country and if the parent who speaks this language to the child sits in just once they have the makings of countless conversations. In such a case, it can be invaluable to follow up the child's DVD encounters with books, audiobooks and even non-linguistic props, such as pillowcases or backpacks featuring the same characters.

If a child is into computer games, try to steer them towards educational games in the minority language, particularly those which train language. There are countless such games, and many children find them extremely useful and entertaining. For older children there are role playing games which involve a good deal of language. Online games will allow the players to interact linguistically with other players, both native and non-native speakers of the minority language. This is, admittedly, particularly easy in the case of English.

Many parents ask relatives in the minority language's country to send books and DVDs rather than toys or clothes when buying presents for the child. It can sometimes be difficult to get hold of materials from abroad. If you have the opportunity to travel to your home country you can search the bookshops for suitable material. We have generally travelled to Ireland or the UK with two empty suitcases, one nested inside the other. They have been full of books and other materials when we went back to Sweden.

For some minority languages it may be possible to buy books and other material by mail order, even via the Internet. Ask around: other families you know or know of may have material their children have grown out of. Public libraries may have some resources. Search for sources of new and used material on the Internet (see the companion website).

Chapter 7

Competence in two cultures

Access to two cultures

Children can be brought up with two languages in any number of different ways. Whether parents have decided that their child should learn a language which neither of them speaks as natives, or whether one or both of them have a minority language which they want to share with their child, they will have to make decisions concerning the culture or cultures which are associated with the language. Knowing a language without being familiar with an associated culture is an academic skill which, while it is valuable in itself, is not always what parents raising their children with two languages had in mind.

Language is often the least of the problems facing a mixed language family. The cultural differences between the parents will often be far more significant. Even where the two cultures involved are ostensibly not far removed from each other, as is the case in the countries of northern Europe or southern Europe, the differences can create major difficulties. For example, the Irish and Swedish ways of doing things may seem to be superficially more similar than different: both countries have Christian traditions, both are agricultural, both have violins and accordions in their folk music, both consume a lot of potatoes, carrots and swedes. Nonetheless, there are thousands of small differences and peculiarities on either side that can lead to misunderstanding and confusion, as well as much amusement. In fact, it is much easier to make allowances for the big differences. It is the small unexpected things that cause problems. Let us take a look at some areas where cultural differences can become important to a family.

Should children brought up bilingually also become bicultural?

The decision to bring up children so that they are familiar with two cultures is not as straightforward as the decision to let them acquire two languages from their parents or others outside or within the home. Children can acquire a language simply by having it spoken to them and being in a situation where they are motivated to use the language for communication. It is far more difficult to arrange for children to acquire knowledge of a culture in the same uncontrived way. While parents alone can give children a second language, they will not be able to give them a second culture without the help of others and the support of society. It is not impossible for a child to acquire knowledge of two cultures, but it requires some work on the part of the parents.

Some families may choose not even to attempt to make their children familiar with the culture associated with the language they speak. Immigrant parents who have become integrated into the majority society may feel no need to pass on the culture they grew up with to their children. The practical difficulties involved may be just too great, especially if the family have little or no contact with others who share the immigrant parent's background. Some immigrant parents may feel that their children need to be fully integrated into the majority society and that any attempt to keep up the ways of the country of origin or to pass on that culture to the children would not be in their interests. Other families have a great need for the children to become familiar with the ways of the 'old country', perhaps for religious reasons.

For families where both parents have a common minority background, the situation is somewhat easier. The minority culture does not have as much competition from the majority culture in the home. Nonetheless, children have contact with the society in which they live through school, friends, sports and other activities. This means that this competition grows as the children get older and become more involved with the world outside the family.

In the case of families where neither parent is a native speaker of the minority language, it is more difficult to familiarise the children with the culture of a country where the language is spoken. Where a minority language or mixed language family can keep the traditions of the minority culture and pass on that culture's ways of looking at the world, any attempt by a majority language family to teach the children the customs of the culture associated with the minority language that one or both of them has chosen to speak with the children may seem contrived. In such a case, it is probably better to rely on frequent trips to a country where the minority language is spoken. In the case of an international language such as English or Spanish, it may not be entirely clear which country's culture might most profitably be associated with the language. There may be no desire at all to have the children become familiar with a culture which is not relevant to any part of their lives. A language like English, Spanish or French will be valuable even if it is disassociated from any kind of cultural context. In many countries with a colonial relationship to a European power and language, there is a value in the language as a language associated with national identity as well as of international communication that is quite separate from the culture of the European country which was originally the source of the language:

> English is important, it is a global language, but it is not enough. You have to try and teach your child the native language. It is very important.
>
> (Grace, a Nigerian in Sweden)

> If a person in Pakistan speaks English we think he is a very educated person. I was four and a half or five when I started English. I could understand the basics of English at that age. That was a good decision my father took, to [help me] learn English at an early age.
>
> (Nazir, Sweden)

> For my daughter the target is English. I really want her to be fluent in English. In the long run maybe she will want to study outside Sweden, maybe in an English-speaking country. If she speaks Swedish now and we travel home, she cannot communicate. If she speaks English perfectly she can communicate alright.
>
> (Anthony, from Sierra Leone, in Sweden)

Parents who want to let their children become familiar with the culture associated with their second (minority) language should think long and hard about how best to go about it, just as they need to do when working out how best to support their children's linguistic development. If the ambition is to let the child later feel as though he or she is equally at home in two countries, more will be required than if the child is only to know how to be polite in the minority parent's country. Either way, the parents can do a great deal at home to prepare the child for visits to the other country.

Feeling at home

Children going to visit, say, grandparents in another country may be very disappointed if they find that there is a lot going on around them which is quite incomprehensible. Even if they have learned their grandparents' language reasonably well and can communicate without too many misunderstandings, they may find that they feel very different from children their own age in their grandparents' country. They might have expected to feel like more than visitors. Parents might expect their children to know intuitively how to behave, as though they should have soaked up such things along with the minority language at home. Mixed language families usually teach their children primarily the manners of the country in which they live. It is questionable whether it is feasible to teach young children two sets of ways to behave. Switching cultural codes is not as easy as switching languages.

An adult brought up with two languages might feel the lack of facility in the culture of the second language even more acutely. It is a sad thing to visit the country in which your mother was brought up and feel like a foreigner. Many families want to avoid their children feeling like foreigners or being perceived by others as foreign in either the country in which they live or the home country of one or both parents. Others may feel that this is not really important. Each family need to make their own decision, but let it be an active decision. Left to themselves, children are unlikely to acquire any culture other than that in which they live and go to school. If they are to feel at home somewhere else as well, it requires an effort by their parents. Some parts of any culture are best learned by children, for example children's books and games which are part of the common background of those who know the culture from the inside. These cannot be learned later instead. Childhood memories are an important part of being a native of a culture. There is much the parent can do to help the child in this respect.

Practice makes perfect. It is unrealistic to think that children can be so well prepared with knowledge about their second culture at home in one country that they will feel immediately at home in another country. The best way to become familiar with the culture of a country is to be in that country as much as possible. From the point of view of acquiring the cultural competence needed to be at home in two cultures, the ideal would be to spend half the year in each country. This would also be an excellent way to learn both languages. However, this is not the way most families choose to live, and such an unsettled way of life would have many other disadvantages, especially for children. But frequent visits to the minority language's country and meeting many different people there, especially other children and their families, will teach the children who live elsewhere much about the way of life. Perhaps they can visit their cousins or their parents' friends if they have children around the same age:

I haven't been in an English-speaking country for a long time. I do feel foreign, but at the same time I feel some kind of bond to the English-speaking world. I'm not completely foreign. I could manage. I know what to do in different situations, but that's more cultural than linguistic.

(Patrik, 18)

German, Dutch and English are closely related so that a real 'culture shock' doesn't occur (well, unless you move to America ...).
(Gabriele Kahn, Oregon)

I make an effort to expose her to other Japanese people around us. Luckily I know some Japanese families (both parents are Japanese) and they often invite me and my daughter to their place. This gives her an opportunity to understand Japanese culture.

(Kaori Matsuda, Australia)

Knowing about the culture builds memories and makes the concepts/words of the minority language come alive and real.

(Andreas Schramm, Minnesota)

Knowing how to behave

Children who grow up in a country learn a great deal about that country's way of life through their own observations, doing as others do, doing what adults tell them, listening to the conversation of adults, watching television and attending school. If children who live in another country come to visit, they may not be aware of the background to what they see around them. If, for example, a child from another country visits a country where terrorist attacks occur from time to time, such as Northern Ireland until fairly recently, bombed out shop fronts and road blocks where armed soldiers point machine guns at cars will probably seem very alarming. Children who visit Sweden may be puzzled by the way people take their shoes off when they go into people's homes, and even certain kinds of public places, such as children's clinics or nursery schools. Children who visit Spain from other countries may be disconcerted when adults they do not know talk to them. Children who visit England may wonder why they are often ignored by adults. Every country has its peculiarities.

Preparing a child for a trip to the minority language country is not easy. Parents will probably want people they visit to think that their children are well brought up. The problem is that being well brought up means different things in different cultures. It is, of course, most important that the children behave appropriately in the country in which they actually live. While at home, the norms of the majority culture may be applied, but the immigrant parent may feel under great pressure to behave according to his or her native culture while visiting the country of origin. This might mean being a lot more strict with the children than normal, which can be very confusing for the children.

In my family, we experienced this several times when we (with two children) were visiting friends in England who also had two children. The children were getting along very well together, if a bit rowdily. Our friends kept hushing their children, obliging us to do the same, although the noise level was a lot less than would usually have been tolerated according to Swedish standards of behaviour.

Religion

Religion and culture are intimately associated with each other. Even in cases when both members of a couple appear to have the same religion, i.e. if they are both Roman Catholics, or both agnostic, or both Muslim, there can be vast differences between the way they view things. A Polish Catholic does not have the same kind of religious life as a French Catholic, nor is a Swedish Lutheran the same as an English Anglican. National characteristics influence the way religion is applied to everyday life. Some societies are more secularised than others.

Religion is not always quite as loaded as it is in Northern Ireland or the Balkans, say, but can nonetheless cause trouble to couples in international relationships. Questions such as whether and where to get married can be problematic; couples may decide not to get married at all. In some countries living together before getting married is not viewed as appropriate. Many parents have breathed a sigh of relief when their adult children decide to get married, whether it is to a 'foreigner' or not.

Getting married in a church or according to the requirements of a religion can be difficult if more than one religion is involved. The couple may have to promise to raise any children in one of their religions before they can get married. There may even be pressure put on one person in the couple to convert to the other's religion. Even if neither of them is religious, they may experience pressure on them to get married in church. For many people, a church wedding is seen as a part of tradition, and a civil ceremony seems like a not very adequate second best. The same is true of baptising children. For some (for example Roman Catholics) baptism is seen as a formal entrance into the

Church; for others (for example many Swedes) baptism is thought of as a traditional naming ceremony with minimal religious significance. A conscious decision not to baptise one's children in Sweden is viewed with utter bafflement by many. In a family where the parents come from different religious traditions the religious upbringing of the children will need to be discussed, particularly if the parents are active in a congregation.

Achieving cultural competence

Children with two languages are often highly motivated to learn appropriate behaviour when they visit the country where the minority language is spoken. They want to fit in and be like everybody else, particularly when they are with other children. They may also be willing to learn new patterns of behaviour to earn the approval of grandparents and other adults.

> **Example**
>
> Leif (8;6) to his grandmother in Ireland: 'In Sweden we say, "Tack för maten" to Pappa and "Thank you for the food" to Mamma, but we can say, "Please may I leave the table?" to you.'

No method of teaching children about the culture of their parent's homeland can ever be as effective as actually taking them there to see for themselves. If the family's ambition is to have the children able to operate like natives of both the languages and cultures involved in their lives, without ever feeling like foreigners, there is a lot they need to learn. This level of competence might never actually be attained, at least not during childhood. This learning process can, however, be begun at home, with the minority language parent telling the children about life in the other country, and making the trappings of childhood in the other country available to the children. Bear in mind that the parent may not be all that well informed about recent developments and changes in society, and may know very little about current trends in childrearing in the home country. Visitors from the country where the minority language is spoken can be a valuable resource for the children. Unfortunately such visitors are often not aware of the family's situation, and may even insist on speaking the majority language to the children. Let us consider some features of what the potentially bicultural child needs to know.

Social behaviour

People in different countries have diverse norms of behaviour. While there are differences between individuals and families, each culture has its own ways. There are all sorts of cultural variations, for example in the way people greet each other and children (kiss, embrace, shake hands, make eye contact, nod, say hello, etc.). They expect different behaviour from children too. Some cultures are much more tolerant of children than others. Problems with this can arise in bicultural families. Even details like how often eye contact is made and how long it is held vary between cultures. Failure to make eye contact as often as expected can give an impression of shiftiness, while overdoing it can be very off-putting for the other person. How loudly and how much a person should speak vary in different cultures, as does how close people stand to each other when talking.

Being polite is another potential area of difficulty for those who need to operate adequately in two cultures. Words like 'please' and 'thank you' do not exist in all languages, and where they do exist they will probably not be used the same way. The German word *bitte* sometimes means 'please' and sometimes not. The Swedish word *tack* can mean 'please' or 'thank you', depending on the context. These words are, however, very important, and taking the time to teach their correct use to the children will do a lot to improve their perceived politeness in the other country. A failure to say 'please' in the English-speaking world can make a child or adult look very rude or foreign in some circumstances. Taxi drivers and ticket collectors can be scathing to any hapless foreigner who forgets to say 'please' and 'thank you' at the appropriate time. My children have reported their Swedish friends commenting on their thanking others unusually frequently.

Religion is an important part of many cultures. Children cannot reasonably be given two religions, but they do need to be aware of the differences between the religion of the 'second' culture as well as the religion of their primary culture. A family where both parents are immigrants from the same place may share the same cultural background and religion and naturally pass it on to their children, even if they live in a country where the majority have a different religion. A mixed couple may have settled for one or the other's religion, or simply not be religious. Religion can be a sensitive matter for grandparents on both sides of the mixed language/culture family. Whatever solution the family comes up with, they risk offending religious sensibilities on one or other side of the family:

Our situation is complicated by the fact that we're Jews; however, the problems that derive from that probably aren't much greater than what they'd have been had we stayed in the USA. Parts of both cultures are virulently anti-Jewish and we've never 'hidden out' in a Jewish community. On both sides of the border, we've always encouraged our children to know what non-Jewish customs are about and to be proud of our own.

(Anonymous, Mexico)

At one time I attended [Christian] 'religious release' classes after school (at the insistence of my third grade teacher and with the approval of my father) and on Sundays attended services at the local Buddhist Temple. In the sixth grade, I declined from attending and my classmates (small K-8 rural school) were a bit shocked when I replied to their inquiry that I was Buddhist but that I had attended in the past because my parents felt all religions were 'good'.

(Fran Schwamm, Japan)

Children growing up with parents from two very different cultures may have difficulty learning much about the culture they do not live in. This is easier with two parents from the same culture, who can together make a home life where their original culture has a strong position. The distances involved or political considerations may make frequent trips to the home country of the parent(s) out of the question. The children may not be able to learn enough about the second culture until they are themselves able to visit that country. In fact it may sometimes turn out that while the parents have created an oasis for their native culture at home, the children are entirely tuned in to the majority culture. This may be a source of conflict in the children's teenage years, if the parents do not permit the children the same freedoms as their friends are allowed:

I went through several phases of cultural adjustment since I have been moving back and forth between USA and Japan quite fre-quently since 17. While I lived in the States from 17 to 21, I tried to become 'American'. I never felt completely comfortable because many of the American characteristics I was trying to incorporate contradicted with what I already had, but at that time, especially when I was attending high school in the countryside, I felt it was the only way to be accepted by peers. I had another difficult time adjusting to new life when I returned to Japan, although I'm not still sure if I was struggling with Japanese culture or with a new school.

(Aya Matsuda, Indiana)

Definitely it has been an advantage to be bilingual, especially since the Chinese language reveals/represents Chinese culture. I identify as multicultural, having a deep appreciation of Chinese values, rituals, even though I grew up in Hollywood, California, in a predominantly Euro-American area. As a child in school, there were awkward experiences of not fitting, not eating American foods, and not being a Christian/familiar with Bible readings, and not fitting the norm.

(Donna May Wong, Oregon)

We have had some discussions of 'our home' being American vs some of the Japanese standards he wants like his classmates. It has never been a 'battle' and he seems to accept it fairly well, as is.

(Fran Schwamm, Japan)

We tended to follow liberal US customs. However, many Mexicans are doing the same, simply because traditional (Hispanic) Mexican childrearing is patriarchal, matricentric and pretty brutal.

(Harold Ormsby L., Mexico)

We took our oldest daughter out of school and home schooled her when she was 10. She is what I consider a 'normal' child – a tomboy who loves to wrestle and climb trees, and doesn't give a hoot for what she's wearing. Well, the girls in her class told her she needed a bra, deodorant and shaved legs – at age 10! Also, she wasn't wearing the right kind of 'cool' clothes, didn't watch TV, didn't participate in the 'Pledge of Allegiance', etc. We are living near a small farming community here where everybody has a gun rack in their pickup trucks. We are currently trying to move to a nearby university town, and I hope we'll have less problems there, being 'different'. I know a German couple in that town, however, whose daughters are also 12 and 10 and refuse to speak German at all because none of their friends are bilingual and they don't want to be 'freaks'. Oh boy. I wish we could find a way to move back to Europe.

(Gabriele Kahn, Oregon)

My parents were quite strict and conservative and I had always believed that this was 'the Japanese way'; however, since living in

Japan for approximately 15 of the last 20 years, I find the Japanese are quite tolerant and indulgent with their children's behaviours.

(Fran Schwamm, Japan)

Children's culture

There is a great deal involved in learning to behave like a native of a country. If bicultural children are to be able to feel like and pass as natives of more than one country when they are adults, then they must experience childhood in both cultures. Having a common background and shared experiences is what being a native of a particular culture is all about. Ideally, this means that the bicultural child should experience at least some of the key parts of childhood in both cultures.

Visiting a school in the second country is an enriching experience if it can be arranged, preferably at several different stages. Might it be possible for the children to go to school with a cousin or a friend's child for a day or two every other year? Such an experience gives children a window on their contemporaries' lives in the second country. They see how the children behave, how the teacher treats them, what they learn and how, and so can compare everything with how things are in their own school. The children's language will also get a boost as they learn words for things which they would never have learned at home: *blackboard, marker, break*, etc.

It is advantageous for a child to experience children's television pro-grammes intended for children of their own age in the second culture. Apart from the language training such programmes give, they also let the child become familiar with the characters and the programmes which their contemporaries will remember fondly when they grow up. It may be possible for programmes to be viewed from another country via the Internet, satellite or cable television, or from DVDs recorded or bought in the second country. Shared experiences are a major part of belonging to any group. Children's literature is equally important. Reading books from both their cultures will help bicultural children to understand the culture better as well as in itself providing an experience the child will have in common with other children in each country.

Parents who are bringing up their children far away from others who share their cultural background may or may not find it natural to sing for their children so that they learn the songs and rhymes of childhood which are part of the culture of the minority language. There are many children's games, songs and even bad jokes which are passed down from older children to younger through the generations in each country. Even if children cannot attend a school in the second country or meet many children from the country, it might be possible to buy a book in which the games are described and teach them to the children.

Traditions

Whether or not to keep the traditions of the second country is a difficult question in many mixed families. Sometimes it may be possible to gather a few compatriots together to celebrate in the traditional manner. Some may settle for sharing the occasion with majority language speakers or just celebrating within the family. It is easy just to let the holiday slip by without being observed. If the majority culture also celebrates the holiday it may be easier to introduce at least some features of the minority culture. From the children's point of view, it is a shame not to share the second culture's traditions with them, even while living in another country.

Special times of year, such as Christmas, New Year, birthdays and the like, often cause all attention to focus on the traditions and customs of the surrounding majority culture. In a family where the parents have different backgrounds and traditions, many questions are raised. Should Christmas be celebrated? If so, and if it is part of the tradition in both countries, should it be celebrated according to the majority tradition or the minority tradition? Many families, particularly if they have young children, choose to celebrate according to both traditions; one country may celebrate on Christmas Eve (for example Sweden) and the other on Christmas Day (for example Ireland), making a two-day feast a reasonable alternative. When my children were younger we celebrated in the Swedish way on Christmas Eve with the Swedish cousins and their families, with cooked ham and meatballs and pickled herring and rice pudding, and then invited them to celebrate with us according to Irish traditions with a turkey or goose and plum pudding on Christmas Day. Some families spend alternate years with each set of grandparents; this usually means that Christmas is celebrated in one or other way each time, but it may be possible to compromise here as so often in an intercultural relationship and take the best of both traditions in a single celebration.

Birthdays can be celebrated in different ways in different countries. Certain birthdays are considered more important than others in some places, such as 18, 21, 40 and 50. In some countries it is considered normal to throw a huge party for everyone you know on certain birthdays (e.g. your 50th birthday in Sweden), while other countries' traditions allow such celebrations to be kept within the family. In some countries, every day of the year is associated with one or more names.

People then celebrate their name days or saint's days on the day which is associated with one of their names. Pity the poor immigrant whose foreign name is not even on the calendar! Mohammed is one of the most common names in Sweden, but it does not have a name day.

In many families it is left up to the women to keep track of birthdays and the like. For women living outside their own culture, the matter of whether or not to give presents or congratulations or send a card on a birthday or name day can be a problem. An immigrant's uncertainty as to the appropriate way to behave can look like indifference or even standoffishness.

Consider which holidays and customs from the minority language culture you feel it is important for your family to celebrate. What do you want to pass on to your children? Some of these holidays may not be celebrated by the majority culture, or not in exactly the same way. It is difficult to celebrate when nobody else is celebrating. Also, you may not have the props for a traditional celebration. Whether Dutch families outside the Netherlands celebrate Sinterklaas in December, or Spanish families outside Spain celebrate the Coming of the Kings in January may depend on how much support parents get from their partner and their children to make the celebration possible. If there is a local immigrant community which shares the same culture, then things get easier. We went to a British–New Zealander Guy Fawkes Party in the depths of the Swedish countryside one year. The local American children near us in Sweden were 'trick or treating' at each other's houses at Halloween long before their Swedish counterparts caught on and started doing the same. Now the Swedish shops are full of American Halloween paraphernalia from mid-October, which makes it nigh on impossible to motivate children to celebrate an Irish Halloween. We have, however, hosted one such memorable event, bonfire, bobbing for apples and all.

> In an effort to teach my children the cultural aspects of their American heritage I have been very conscious of celebrating all American holidays (Thanksgiving, Halloween, St Patrick's Day, Valentine's Day, 4th of July and Christmas, of course, with all its typical cultural characteristics).
>
> (Margo Arango, Colombia)

> We celebrate Christmas the Czech way rather than the American way, which my husband and I felt was too commercialised. (The austere Communist Christmases in Czechoslovakia had this influence on me.) Even though my son is now 24 and my daughter 18,

they still look forward to their Christmas stockings from St Nicholas and getting their gifts from Baby Jesus. We had to devise a sort of family mythology to explain the existence of Santa Claus – he had to take care of American kids, he was really Baby Jesus' helper, etc. But there was also a blending of American and Czech customs, as we adjusted to life in this country.

(Althea Pribyl, Oregon)

Since all of our family and extended families spend holidays toge-ther, everyone is exposed to Chinese culture – food, art, language, clothing. On the whole, all of us see multilingualism as an asset and something to achieve to enhance relationships and communication within our diverse society.

(Donna May Wong, Oregon)

Hospitality

The way guests are treated and prepared for is another potential source of conflict in the intercultural family. On hearing that they are to have guests, the couple may react totally differently: one may be concerned with finding time to clean the house from top to bottom lest the visi-tors think it dirty, while the other may immediately start planning menus; one may want to get the kitchen painted before the visitors come, while the other may wish to get a bigger, more expensive-looking TV set; one may be worried about not having matching towels, while the other is more concerned with how much wine the visitors are likely to drink. While some of these differences reflect individual interests, there are cultural patterns at work too, regulating how we want others to perceive us.

Guests to a Swedish home are expected to take their shoes off and walk around in their socks except at the most formal parties, where they will often bring indoor shoes to wear, particularly in winter. This tradition is of course due to the unsuitable combination of bare polished wooden or vinyl floors with rag rugs and wet or snowy footwear, but really the climate is no wetter than in England, say, where the combi-nation of wet or muddy outdoor shoes and soft absorbent carpeting is quite unhygienic. Failure to observe the appropriate customs can cause as much resentment in one country as in the other. Woe betide dinner guests to an English home who try to take their shoes off, or visitors in Sweden who walk in with their shoes on, leaving pools of water on the floor! Nothing might be said, it being known that the offender is a foreigner, but if looks could kill …

Away from home too, out at the pub or a restaurant, the matter of who pays for what varies in different cultures. Some never allow a woman to pay for anything, others 'go Dutch': even the expression reflects a cultural difference. Some have a culture of 'buying rounds', with strict turn–taking rules, while others have everybody counting out their own share of the bill, even at a restaurant. Failure to be aware of the appropriate behaviour can cause resentment and a breakdown in communication.

These differences are part of the adult culture and very difficult to teach explicitly. In addition, these kinds of unwritten rules are liable to change as years go by, so parents who have not lived in their native culture for many years may be quite old–fashioned in their behaviour. The best way for children and young people to prepare for a period in the 'other' country is to be aware that things will be different from what they are at home and to keep their eyes and ears open and do what others do. This advice is, of course, appropriate for any young people going abroad. The difference is that youngsters who have grown up with the language spoken in the country they are going to visit may speak the language with little or no foreign accent or lack of fluency and therefore be expected to behave like native speakers.

Food and drink

Food and drink can be a source of difficulty for the family with two cultures. In southern Europe, for example, it is considered perfectly normal for even quite young children to drink wine mixed with water. In Scandinavia such a practice would be considered scandalous and might even be illegal. In some countries, the evening meal is served very late, and children stay up late at night, while people in other countries eat much earlier and have children in bed by 7 or 8 p.m. The kinds of food served may be very characteristic of the culture. Mixed families often come up with a compromise on the question of what kind of food they eat, taking favourites from each tradition. The children may well be used to the food eaten in both the country they live in and the country that one parent comes from. This is because immigrants often miss the food they are used to and see to it that they can at least sometimes eat the familiar dishes of their childhood. In doing so, they automatically pass on the culinary tradition of their home country to their children. There may be some things that you feel it is important to pass on to your children. My children, for example, have been brought up with jelly and ice cream at birthday parties, to the amazement (and sometimes disgust) of their Swedish friends, and occasional feeds of Irish potato bread, also called fadge, which is very popular even with Swedes!

Eating and drinking are major parts of the culture of a people, and this is certainly reflected in the daily life of the intercultural couple. If only one of them shops and cooks, more of that side's culinary tradition may be represented, but not necessarily. Many families find that their eating habits gravitate towards a mixture of food from the majority and the minority culture, at least if it is the immigrant who does the cooking. Otherwise there will probably be a lot more majority culture food.

Many people really learn to cook only when they set up house on their own, and if that is in a country other than where they were brought up, then that will be reflected in the food they eat. For an immigrant with a partner from the majority culture, much can be learned about the majority culture's food. You need to learn to shop for food in a new way: even if you might be able to find enough familiar food from your home country, it will be imported and therefore expensive. You may have to learn to eat like the people of the majority culture if your grocery bills are not to get out of control. This is not to say that you need to totally turn your back on the cooking methods and ingredients you are familiar with, but you may need to adapt recipes to locally available foodstuffs, and save authentic specialities from your childhood for special occasions.

Men and women

In all cultures, even those which profess to have totally gone beyond any kind of gender-bound thinking, the relationship between men and women is fundamental, but it works differently in different cultures. While women in some countries may feel financially and socially obliged to work full time outside the home and leave their toddlers in day-care, women in other countries are financially and socially able to and are expected to stay at home with their children until they start school. Men in such settings may find that this option is not open to them. The intercultural family's expectations of how men and women behave are not always met.

Men and women have different areas of responsibility in different cultures, although individual differences may be considerable: potential areas of conflict may include childcare, cooking, housework, practical house repair work, shopping for food and clothes and economic responsibility. These issues are sensitive, and difficult to discuss for many people, although they will be important in connection with the way the children are to be raised. The family may need to be aware of cultural differences between what they see, for example, as boys' and girls' education, chores, pastimes and toys. For some fathers it may be important that they are able to pass on to their sons knowledge given them by their fathers, be it about football, how to tickle a trout, how to put up wallpaper or how to judge which trees in a forest to fell first. Mothers may have similar knowledge to pass on to their daughters, about traditional crafts, how to make traditional foodstuffs or traditional ways of dressing.

There are, however, advantages to growing up in an intercultural family. It is a way to learn about other people and to understand that there is really very little that can be taken for granted. The adults involved also come to see their own culture through new eyes, and may become more broadminded in the process. It is not for everybody. Anybody looking for a simple life would do much better to marry the boy or girl next door! Many adults who themselves grew up with two languages report mixed experiences of being exposed to two cultures:

> I think I fit into other cultures better since I have practical, almost daily experience of moving from one to another.
>
> (Jasmin Harvey, USA)

> For me, being multicultural has meant that I'm not clearly 'from' anywhere; not that that's a problem, necessarily. When I was a college student here in the States, I found the questions and comments of my monocultural peers unbearably predictable (cute accent, there was an exchange student from Finland in my high school, etc.). There isn't a convenient category people can plug me in, so in those early years I tended to find myself repeating my entire weird family history over and over to near strangers – or even total strangers. Now I just don't do that for them; if someone must know 'where I'm from' I tell some convenient part of the story. I'm not obligated to help them categorise me. Lately, I've managed to blend in, so most people don't realise how strange my background is.
>
> (Mai Kuha, USA)

Chapter 8

Problems you may encounter

Quality of input

If children are to acquire two languages they need to hear enough of both languages spoken directly to them (i.e. sitting a child in front of a television programme in the target language will not generally be enough). But if children are regularly spoken to by non-native speakers of the language they will probably pick up features of their speech. Some parents are concerned about speaking their non-native language in front of the children (even if not speaking directly to the children) lest the children pick up non-native characteristics from the parent's speech. In the case of the minority language parent speaking the majority language, there is probably no need to worry. Most children hear so many native speakers of the majority language that they will probably not use any erroneous pronunciations, words or grammar that they pick up from their minority language parent. Even if a small child copies a parent's foreign accent in the majority language, this will generally be replaced by a local accent as the child's social circle grows.

In the case of the minority language, it might be better for children to hear even non-native speakers if this means that they also hear more native speech in the minority language. In other words, the child will hear the minority language-speaking mother more often if she speaks her language both directly to the child and also when she speaks to the child's father. This more than makes up for the possibility of the child picking up the father's foreign accent in the minority language. Our experience is that children soon become aware of which parent makes mistakes in a language and will join the native-speaking parent in pointing out errors.

Losing a language

Even the parent who is a native speaker of a language may not always be an error-free language model. After years without much contact

with other native speakers, particularly native speakers who do not
know the majority language, you might feel that your proficiency in
your first language is no longer what it was. Unusual words may have
disappeared from your active vocabulary and even from your passive
vocabulary. Doing crosswords or playing Scrabble with friends from
your youth who stayed at home can be a real eye-opener, and may
make you realise just how far behind your advanced vocabulary has
fallen.

The speech of those who have lived abroad for many years is sometimes quaint and full of out-of-date expressions. Words referring to
technological advances are also problematic; you may know them well
enough in the language of your new country, but how do you say
them in your native language? The same goes for experiences you have
had in your new language, such as having a baby or learning a sport:
you can say it all in the new language, but you may just not have the
appropriate vocabulary in your native language. For example, are car
windows toned or tinted? Do you leave your children in day-care or
childcare or what?

> Of course my first language is affected! I speak a much simpler
> English than before. Sometimes I just cannot find that one word
> that eludes me. ... Part of me now views people with extensive
> vocabularies as pretentious and the other part of me is jealous.
>
> (American woman living in Sweden)

> Fortunately I use Japanese at work. This helps a lot to preserve my
> language skill. However, my Japanese has 'frozen' since I left Japan
> nine years ago. If I speak to people in Japan now my Japanese may
> sound slightly out of date.
>
> (Kaori Matsuda, Australia)

Once you have become proficient in your second language, you may
find that the patterns of that language pervade your thinking and the
way you plan what to say next. You may say something which superficially appears to be in your native language, and which may go
unnoticed if you are speaking to others who share your linguistic
situation or to native speakers of the majority language, but which a
monolingual speaker of your native language might totally fail to
understand. In this case, you have probably made a direct translation of
an idiom of the majority language without recognising it as such. You
are in an even worse situation than a native speaker of the majority
language, who would probably avoid trying to translate such idioms

into another language. Your use of such constructions in your so-called native language will legitimise them in the eyes of your children.

There is evidence to suggest that it is not possible to become native-like in a second language without cost to your first language. Major (1990) studied American women who had lived in Brazil for many years. He found that the better their pronunciation of Portuguese, the greater the effect on their pronunciation of English. Major measured tiny differences in the way that the women pronounced <t>, <d> and <k> in English and Portuguese in both formal and casual speech. The women were in fact starting to pronounce English consonants in a way that was not quite American and not quite Portuguese, almost as though they were developing tendencies towards Portuguese accents in their English.

Any effect that a majority language has on an immigrant's native language is intrinsically undesirable. This is particularly so when immigrants are trying to pass on their native language to their children and the target is to have the child become proficient in the language as it is spoken in the parent's country of origin. However, even less than perfectly native input is infinitely better than none.

What to do about language attrition?

I posted a question to the Internet mailing list TESL-L for teachers of English as a second language (which actually has many members who are involved in teaching English as a foreign language, i.e. not in a country where English is spoken) asking what members of the list did to keep from losing their English while living abroad. The 25 answers gave many helpful tips:

- Several people recommended listening to radio broadcasts in English, and reading books and magazines.
- One had relatives send clippings from newspapers and magazines with examples of current slang and idiom.
- Another felt that his English might actually have improved while abroad since teaching and translation work focuses attention on the language.
- An American in Turkey felt that the lack of contact with native speakers in combination with teaching English had produced a hyper-correct form of English (with, for example, overly clear enunciation).
- Several replies pointed out the value of British and American television shows for gleaning current usage.

- Some people suggested trying to find newcomers, who are still uninfluenced by the majority language, or speakers of English as a second language who have a language other than the majority language as their first language.
- One American who has been living in France for the past 25 years reported that he tries to think as though he was at home, for example when he answers the phone he says what he would have said if he had never left home. He also advised answering in English any-body who speaks English to you, even if their English is poor, making no allowance for their difficulties: 'We're not in class now!' he wrote.
- Another English speaker who has lived in France for over 20 years reported being less than thrilled when he was complimented in Canada on how well he spoke English. He recommended listening to the radio and reading, as well as keeping a vocabulary book to learn neologisms and forgotten metaphors.
- Reading English books aloud to your children and doing crosswords were other recommendations, as well as reading recent novels.
- Many replies pointed out that just being aware of the problem was half the battle.

> I am very grateful to my children for allowing me to continue with my native language on a daily basis. I am sure it would have severely suffered otherwise. I can only take what the English only (or mainly) environment does to my academic German as an indi-cation of what would happen to my 'private' German if it wasn't for them.
>
> (Susanne Dopke, Australia – author of *One Parent, One Language: An Interactional Approach*, 1992)

> My German has considerably deteriorated through the continuous use of English. This became apparent when in 1983 my father read something I had written in German and published. He corrected all the syntax and punctuation, as well as some aspects of vocabulary. The mistakes were recognisable to me and a clear indication of how much I had lost the accuracy of my German.
>
> (German man living in England)

Semilingualism

The term semilingual is sometimes used to refer to individuals, often second generation immigrants, who are said to lack native-speaker competence in either of their languages. Skutnabb-Kangas (1981) and

Hansegard (1975) are associated with the term 'semilingualism'. This is the worst case scenario that haunts many parents who are bringing up their children with two languages. Romaine (1995: 261–65) explains how the notion developed in connection with the study of the language skills of ethnic minorities. Semilingualism implies a comparison with some kind of idealised full competence in a language. Romaine explains this view in terms of what she calls 'the container view of competence' (1995: 264). An ideal adult monolingual speaker has a 'full container', while an ideal adult bilingual has two full containers; a semilingual adult has two less than full containers. She relates this to Lambert's (1975) notion of the balanced bilingual, i.e. one who has equal though not necessarily full knowledge of two languages. The notion of semilingualism has been dismissed by researchers as being due to a mistaken view of cognitive development, and partly due to the techniques used to test the linguistic development of children with two languages. The discussion has concerned speakers in bilingual communities rather than the kind of individual bilingual situation I describe in this book.

The notion of semilingualism has generally been rejected. It is, nonetheless, very common for children who grow up with two languages to have difficulty in the minority language (for example foreign accent, limited vocabulary, non-native grammar, etc.). This is usually due to their limited exposure to the minority language, and will generally improve if they are in a situation with more input in that language. Some of these children might have subtle problems with the majority language, for example with gaps in their vocabulary. This cannot, however, be attributed solely to the child's bilingual situation. Most children find ways to compensate for not hearing the majority language in all kinds of situations, for example through their majority language schoolwork and social contacts or in their own reading. But children who avoid reading and who do not do well in school for reasons unconnected to their linguistic situation may be left with a less than monolingual-like command of the majority language. Of course, it is impossible to know how an individual's command of the majority language would have been if he had never been exposed to a minority language.

Most parents, teachers and linguists would agree that it is absolutely essential for the children who grow up with two languages to have at least one language which they know very well. It is often assumed that the majority language must necessarily be the dominant language. This is certainly the usual way, and probably most advantageous to the child who is being schooled through the medium of the majority language.

If the child is being educated in the minority language at home or at an international school, then that language may be dominant. It is generally expected that the dominant language at least will be mastered without any foreign accent and in every other way be equivalent to a monolingual's native language.

For some second generation immigrant youngsters in the inner cities things do not work out this way: they end up sounding non-native in both their languages. Research in Sweden (Kotsinas 1994) indicates that a new variety of Swedish may, in fact, be emerging, spoken by young people who live in areas of Swedish cities where native Swedish speakers are a tiny minority and many languages are spoken. Swedish becomes a lingua franca, but, with few native speakers around to model it, the language develops in new directions, borrowing words from many different immigrant languages. This is not to say that these speakers cannot or do not also learn standard Swedish.

For a small number of children, even those brought up with two languages in circumstances which would appear to favour the majority language, the second or minority language may influence the dominant or majority language. Children with two languages have quite simply more to learn. If these children are to have a satisfactory command of at least one and preferably both of their languages, both the children and the parents, and ideally also the children's teachers, will have to work at it. Those well-meaning strangers who comment on how great it is that the children get a second language for free do not know what they are saying. Of course, all children do not have problems. Very many parents and teachers feel that their children are indistinguishable from monolingual children in their dominant (majority) language.

Changed circumstances

For one reason or another, things do not always go according to plan. No matter how well a couple thought through how they wanted to handle their child's linguistic development with two languages, things do not always turn out as they expected. People move away, get divorced, or die, thwarting the bilingual family's arrangements. In some cases external events may play havoc with the lives of individuals. Perhaps employment or domestic matters force a family to move to another country or to move back to a country where one or both of the parents came from. This means that they may need to modify their plans and targets for their children's language acquisition. A family moving back to the country where both parents originate from must decide whether they will try to maintain their children's (and indeed their own) level of competence in the majority language of the country they are leaving. If they are going on to another overseas position where there will be a new language and culture to learn, most will probably put their language skills to work to help them learn the new language, rather than try to maintain a language that they no longer need in their daily life.

A family who is not likely to live abroad again may try to keep up the children's language. One way to do this is by employing an au pair from that country. A couple I knew, both from Northern Ireland, had lived many years in Sweden and finally left to live in England with their three children (all born in Sweden). They were unsure whether they would want to return to Sweden or not, and wanted to keep their options open. They came up with the ingenious scheme of bringing one of the helpers at their children's Swedish pre-school back with them to England as an au pair.

Divorce

There is no shortage of reasons why a mixed language, intercultural couple might come into conflict with each other. The odds are really stacked against them. In addition to their cultural differences, linguistic confusion may compound the partners' lack of common ground with misunderstandings and misinterpretations of what the other says and an inability to express themselves so the other can read both the message and what is written between the lines. However, both partners go into the relationship with their eyes open, even if love is blind. They are likely to be aware of the problems; the only issue is whether they can find ways to live with them or whether they allow the difficulties of an intercultural relationship to overshadow the advantages.

The breakdown of any relationship can be a tragedy for those involved. In the intercultural relationship, the stakes may be higher. If one partner has left his or her home country to move to the other's country, what is that partner to do if the relationship collapses? Depending on the terms of the particular country's immigration legislation, the foreign partner may or may not be allowed to stay in the new country. (In Sweden, for example, a permanent residence permit is usually granted to love-immigrants after three years – before that they must leave if the relationship ends.) If it is possible to stay in the country, the immigrant is faced with a number of decisions. The individual circumstances of the immigrant's work and the possibility of getting work in the home country will presumably influence the decision.

The real problems start when there are children involved. They may not have any interest in being uprooted and moving to their mother's or father's country of origin and away from any possibility of reasonable access to the other parent. An immigrant parent who decides to stay in the other parent's country will need to make a new life alone or with the children. This can be difficult if the native partner has been the one to deal with the authorities and the family's administration; however, many native divorcees are in a similar position.

For some, it may not be possible to return to their country of origin. This might be because they have relinquished their original nationality to adopt that of their new country, so that they no longer have any right of residence in their country of origin. Others may feel that they have been away from their original country for so long that it no longer feels like home. Some may come from cultures where the stigma of being divorced is so great that it makes a life in exile appear to be a more attractive option. For those who left their home country against the wishes of their parents, going back after the relationship's breakdown might feel like the ultimate failure and loss of face.

Other problems arise for the children of a mixed language couple who get divorced. If the minority language-speaking parent no longer lives with the children it may be difficult for them to get enough input in the minority language. This is especially true if the minority language-speaking parent moves back to his or her country of origin. Even making trips to the minority parent's new home may not be enough to let the children continue their bilingual development. However, if the trips are frequent and long enough these children may be better able to acquire both languages and cultures than they would have been if their parents had not divorced. They can see both languages in the context of their associated cultures; both parents are fully linguistically and culturally competent. The children see both cultures and languages at their best:

> My two older children still speak Dutch with their father, whom they see for about six weeks each year, and we read Dutch books together, and sometimes I speak Dutch with them. They haven't lost their fluency so far.
>
> (Gabriele Kahn, Oregon)

> I had to fight hard to get the children for as many as 12 days a month (every Tuesday night, and from Thursday night to Sunday night, twice a month). One of my principal motivations was to

establish a regular English language and cultural environment for them.

(Sean Golden, Barcelona)

If it is the majority language-speaking parent who moves away from the children, the position is different. The minority language-speaking parent may wish to return to the country of origin, taking the children along. The other parent may oppose such a move on the grounds that his or her relationship with the children would be made very difficult. The children might forget the language if they move to a country where they have no contact with speakers of that language. Otherwise, if the minority language-speaking parent remains in the country the family lived in before the divorce, he or she will be left with a monolingual minority language home. In some cases, this might strengthen the children's minority language skills, but it is unlikely to be generally beneficial to the children, given the reduced amount of time that single parents are generally able to spend with their children.

In some cases it has happened that minority language parents have taken the children away to their home country against the will of the other parent, even if they did not have custody of the children. Sometimes these cases are brought to trial as kidnapping, and parents can be denied any access to their children for many years. These extreme breakdowns in the relationship between parents are presumably more likely to occur when there are significant cultural and religious differences.

Death of a parent

The death of a parent while a child is growing up is always tragic, especially for young children. In addition to all the other effects it will have, a parent's death in a mixed language family may result in severe problems with the children's linguistic development, especially in the case of the loss of the minority language-speaking parent. This language may suddenly disappear from the children's lives. In such a case, visits to grandparents and cousins in the deceased parent's home country are valuable and may be a way forward for the children. Much depends on how old they are when they lose their parent.

In the event of the majority parent's remarriage, unexpected challenges may arise, especially if the new spouse is a fellow native of the country of residence. Children who are used to a certain kind of upbringing and cooking may not have realised how much their way of life was influenced by their deceased parent's foreign culture. They may be surprised to be exposed to an undiluted dose of the majority culture at home, and miss their other parent's language and ways almost as much as they miss the parent. Most mixed language families live a life which has features of both traditions. The children may not be able to maintain their minority language skills in such a situation, unless their other parent is very motivated to help them.

Adjusting to setbacks

Some children may simply be frustrated by the whole idea of two languages, like the little boy in the following comment:

> I was raised speaking French and English in Brooklyn, NY. My parents spoke French at home, and we learned English in school and with our peers. My brother tried to raise his children bilingually, but his son, at the age of four, rejected the whole idea by yelling once: 'The words, they're stuck in my throat, they won't come out.'
>
> (Helene Ossipov, Arizona)

Children with one, two or more languages go through any number of phases in their use of their languages as in other aspects of their development. A major problem at the age of three may have completely disappeared by 3;6, replaced by another new problem; children's developmental phases do not last forever. The parents in the above example gave up their attempt to let the child acquire French, one of his father's two languages. They may or may not have made a wise choice: only the parents are really in a position to decide what is best for their child. There are, however, a number of ways to help children get over a temporary problem.

The most important way to help your children is to ensure that they get as much input as possible in both languages. Another way to help is to be consistent in who speaks which language, especially at the beginning. A child will find it easier to sort out the two languages if there is some logic behind the choice of which language is used. Later on, many parents feel that they do not have to be quite as consistent and may, for example, speak the majority language to the child when guests are present.

Many parents find that their children sooner or later begin to answer them in the majority language, even when addressed in the minority language. This is not a reason to give up, just a minor and temporary setback. There are several methods that parents have used successfully to thwart this majority language intrusion. Probably the most effective way is to take the children to a country where they will hear only the minority language for a week or two, preferably without taking a majority language-speaking parent along! This is often enough to turn things around and restore the child–parent dialogue in the minority language. Other methods which we have found useful, but which may or may not help, are the following:

- Remind the child to speak the minority language. Often children are just so eager to say what they have on their minds that they are unwilling to take the time or make the effort to use the minority language, which is probably their weaker language. A gentle prompt might be enough to encourage them back to the minority language.
- Repeat back what the child said but using the minority language, in much the same way as a parent corrects and expands the speech of a much younger child. For example, if the child says in Swedish, 'Får jag åka och bada med Niklas?' (Can I go swimming with Niklas?) to his mother, with whom he is 'supposed' to speak English, the mother might say, 'Do you want to go swimming with Niklas?'
- An alternative is to refuse to answer the child until he or she uses the appropriate language. This will not be a suitable tactic for some children, and should be used in a spirit of fun rather than force.
- A milder variant is to say in the appropriate language something like 'Sorry, what was that you said?' This should not be taken too far. Some children will become thoroughly frustrated if they are not allowed to express themselves in the language of their choice. It might work to wear down the child's resistance by, as often as seems reasonable, reacting when they use the 'wrong' language, but not going on at them about it, and not refusing to listen to what they are trying to say. Children need to feel that they can talk to their parents. You know your child, do what you think will work!

> Kids will become as proficient as they need to be, and no more, in both languages. Language proficiency can be increased at any point in life.
>
> (Harold Ormsby L., Mexico)

> My only advice to others is to do what feels natural. Don't follow anyone else's advice.
>
> (Nancy Holm, Sweden)

Remember that some kids may well not want to be bilingual. It is, after all, a personal decision. They may be happy enough to know another language (anyway, once a language is in your head, you can't get it out) but they may not want to use it. In general, these kids will prefer the language of the society around them. In some cases, this may be 'a phase'; in others, it may be a decision for life. In either case, I think parents should respect the kid's decision.

(Harold Ormsby L., Mexico)

Redefining targets

Eventually, some parents find that they are obliged to lower the level of ambition they had at the beginning concerning their child's bilingual development. If they had envisaged a balanced bilingual with mono-lingual-like knowledge of two languages and cultures, they may find that their child by the age of 10 is a monolingual-like speaker of the majority language with some level of knowledge of the minority language. Even if the child is reluctant to speak the minority language, an extensive passive knowledge can be maintained if the parent perseveres with speaking the minority language to the child as often as possible. This passive knowledge can be built upon at a later stage. If the child is at all willing to use the minority language, the parents can feel very pleased with themselves.

Even speech full of interference from the majority language is an invaluable asset to the child, allowing them access to the minority language-speaking side of the family, as well as the associated culture. Such a child has the potential to become very competent in their second language given an opportunity to use it in a setting where it is the majority language. The key to success is not to give up, even in the face of adversity, and to adapt to changes in the way that is most beneficial to the child:

> Well, I can actually remember that time [when I first felt proficient in Italian]. It was around 12 or 13 years old. We went to Italy for three months. I was playing in the village with my cousins and I was one of the gang. I understood them and they understood me, and at some point they said, 'Loretta, you really speak good Italian.'
>
> (Loretta, Sweden)

Children with special needs

Other setbacks to the parents' plans may arise if they find that one or more of their children has a specific difficulty with languages. Children are individuals, and some learn language more easily than others. Some children may have special needs, such as hearing deficiencies or developmental disorders. Parents of these children may need to re-evaluate their position, and perhaps modify the targets they have more or less consciously set up for their children's linguistic and general development.

On an intuitive level you might feel that children born from the genetic melting pot of a mixed marriage should be extraordinarily healthy individuals. Unfortunately there is no guarantee of this: disabled children are born in families with two languages just as in families with a single language. There are many disabilities that can affect children's ability to deal with language, for example deafness, Down's Syndrome, dyslexia, attention deficit hyperactivity disorder (ADHD), autism and other learning difficulties.

Deaf children are nowadays usually taught sign language as their first language, and may subsequently learn something of the mainstream majority spoken language (at least in its written form). They are thus brought up bilingually in sign language and the spoken language. In a family where more than one language is spoken, arrangements may have to be made to allow the deaf child to concentrate on a single spoken language. Two languages to be acquired in addition to sign language is probably an unrealistic target without the benefit of hearing. The family need to decide which of the spoken languages the child will use more. If the family do not intend to move, the majority language is likely to be more useful to the child in daily dealings with the health services and aides. If the family plan to move to another country in the future, for example back to the parents' homeland, they might need to rethink, or to bring the move forward in time, to save the deaf child from a language switch. Similar problems are faced by parents of children with other disabilities.

Examples

An English-speaking couple were living in Sweden when their first child was born with Down's Syndrome. Both parents spoke English to the child in the beginning, and she learned some Swedish at her day-care and in the course of all the various therapy sessions she attended. Eventually the family intended to return to England, but they returned earlier than planned to spare their daughter the additional complication of bilingualism. These children have enough to cope with in one language. It seems unnecessary to burden them with two. But there are families and children for whom there is no alternative but to battle on with two or more languages.

A child in a mixed language (English–Swedish) family has autism. His language delay was considerable in both languages. At the age of two he used only a few words (mixed Swedish and English). When he was three his English was clearly dominant; much of his language was taken from DVDs. In fact, he used only English in his communication outside the family, for example to his pre-school teachers. By the age of six his Swedish had taken over (and had actually caught up so that his language was very nearly normal for his age). At that time he understood English well, but would generally answer in Swedish. He got away with this without pressure to speak English, but he was fully aware that he would need to speak English when he visited his grandparents. The family persevered with the one person–one language method with him, as with their other children, and are now satisfied that that was the best solution for him and for the entire family. By age 10 he began using both languages appropriately.

Seeing the signs

Some children are late talkers. This is true of children growing up with one, two or more languages. It may be the case for some children that their language delay is caused by having two languages. The children are expected to learn twice as much, but given the same total amount of stimulation and help from their parents. Language delay usually means that the child is trying to make rules for the way the languages work. There is no evidence that this kind of delay has any long-term effects on the child's speech.

It is, nonetheless, important to be just as observant about a lack of speech or other problem with language development in a child exposed to two languages as in any other child, and have the child's hearing and development checked if you are worried. Do not let yourself be reassured by other parents who tell you about children they have known (with or without two languages) who did not speak until they were much older than your child and who went on to speak beautifully. If you are concerned about your child's language development, do have the child checked up. If there is no need to be concerned, it will put your mind at rest, but some late-talking children do have hearing or other developmental problems. The earlier these conditions are discovered the better.

Chapter 9

Keeping it up

Motivation

The single most important factor in raising children with two languages (as, indeed, in any other language learning situation) is motivation. Without a good reason, the effort required to learn a language is simply not worth making. Children, at least after a certain age, need to be motivated to accept being spoken to in the minority language and to make the attempt to answer their parent in this language. Parents need to be motivated, at first to accommodate their children into the couple's language system in such a way that they will be systematically exposed to both languages, and later to ensure that they get sufficient direct interaction in each language. Both the parents and the children will find that their levels of motivation will fluctuate. One or other parent may spend less time with the children than the other; the children may be away from home most of the time. A parent who is himself trying to learn the majority language may well want to use it as much as possible, even with his children. The family language system must be flexible enough to adapt to the family's changing circumstances. If the system breaks down for any reason, for example a change in the family's country or even city of residence, a divorce or bereavement, a new system must be devised to replace it:

> I do feel guilty. I wonder just how selfish I was, bringing them up speaking Galician and Spanish. Because I wanted to better my own skills. How much was it an unconscious selfish decision of mine to not speak English as often as I could. It nags at you sometimes. I have a colleague who is a Londoner. He is married to a Galician woman who is an English teacher. They both spoke English to their son – he's 13 now. But his Spanish was picked up from his everyday relationships. So now he is perfectly bilingual in Spanish

and English. I don't know if he has any Galician. My kids are not. But they are both very aware of language as a social factor.

(David, Galicia)

Promote children's self-image as speakers of the minority language

A belief in oneself is a powerful tool. Children who are encouraged in their use of the minority language and praised for their proficiency will quickly come to see themselves as speakers of that language. They may, of course, be disappointed when they realise that they are not actually indistinguishable from monolingual peers, but they are much more likely to want to communicate in the minority language if they believe that they do it well. The converse is, naturally, also true. Children who are corrected overly often or teased for making mistakes in the minority language will be reluctant to speak it and will be unsure of their ability to communicate using the language. Such children may well turn their backs entirely on the second language:

> But I have it in me, and when I went to Italy now with my friends. I impressed myself after a day or two. It's there! But the fact that I learned a third language put it on hold. And I haven't practised it since my mother died, more than 12 years ago now.

> (Loretta, Sweden)

Work systematically with your children

If your children are not getting any help with their minority language in the community or their school, you may want to support them in an academic way at home. For pre-school children you may be able to find early learning books produced to let monolingual parents and children practise concepts such as reading, writing, counting and colours in the minority language.

With children from the age of seven or eight you may want to work through the kinds of material that children use in their language work in a country where the minority language is spoken. If you can find a way to motivate your children to study their weaker language, this kind of work can be valuable. Perhaps you can contact teachers in your home country and ask what books they recommend. You may need to use books meant for slightly younger children. Most children with two languages are not quite up to the level of their monolingual peers in the minority language. If you can get hold of books intended for home schooling, these might be suitable. You may like to set up a regular time for the child to work with you in the minority language, maybe for a couple of hours on Saturday or Sunday mornings, and then again for a couple of hours on the evening they have least homework. If you have more than one schoolchild, let them study the minority language together. They might not make a class, but they can work together on some things. Avoid competition between them if that is a problem.

It can be difficult to make this kind of extra study at home work without some external motivation or target. I have personally had only sporadic success on this front, generally on the children's own initiative after they have been in Ireland or in some other situation where they have seen the benefit of proficiency in English. Their enthusiasm has soon waned when they realise how much they have to learn. Other parents I know have been better able to regularly home school their children in the minority language. How important you feel this is will depend on your family situation and your children's inclinations and abilities.

Teenagers

As children grow older they may be less likely to want to speak the minority language. Pleasing a parent is, for many young people, no longer sufficient motivation for making an extra effort or being different. If the minority language is a school language, both young people who have grown up with the language and their schoolmates may see the value of being proficient, although some may find that being better than the rest of the class is an embarrassment in itself. One of the major advantages we have found with bilingual and English-medium education is that all the children in the class are in the same boat – speaking English is not 'different' in such an environment.

Using the minority language

Some parents find that while they were able to give their children the kind of linguistic input they needed to learn to speak the minority language when they were young, there comes a point where they are not able to develop their language further. The level of language proficiency expected of a young adult is simply more than it is possible to achieve in a setting where the language is represented by a single parent or a handful of speakers. If young people are to develop their language further it will have to be through contacts with other speakers of the language. Some of these contacts can be one way, for example through the written word in newspapers, magazines and books or through radio and television programmes in the minority language. Newspapers and magazines can be subscribed to or are available through the Internet. Books in many languages can be bought (for example via the Internet) or borrowed from libraries. TV and radio in the minority language may be available via satellite, cable or the Internet.

If a young person who has actively used the minority language suddenly stops and chooses to answer the minority language-speaking parent in the majority language, it is worth attempting to reverse this decision. There are several approaches which might work:

- What kind of career does the young person envisage? There may be some way to associate the desired career with the minority language. A young person who dreams of being, for example, a journalist has two markets for her work if she has sufficient facility in two languages. Perhaps you could help such youngsters to access magazines and papers in the minority language (possibly through the Internet) to show that there are speakers of the minority language who share their interests. If, for example, a career in banking is the goal, knowledge of two languages and cultures is an asset. A prospective teacher can either teach in a country where the minority language is spoken or be a resource for the pupils with two languages in the majority language country. A young person who plans to work in tourism or other service jobs will find the minority language useful sooner or later.
- What are your teenager's interests? Is it possible to put them in touch with peers who share the same interests in a country where the minority language is spoken?
- The ultimate motivation for using a language is to need it to communicate. Would it be possible to send your teenager to the country where the minority language is spoken? This could be to go to school or college there for a period, to work, for example for a summer job, or just to visit relations or friends there.
- In the case of English, I have motivated a 10-year-old to read English books (with the help of printed and audiobooks) by pointing out that a native-like command of the language is within his grasp. I also mentioned that being a native speaker of English (in combination with a good general education) is enough to live on in many parts of the world.
- Consider bribery or reward schemes, or anything you can think of.

Even if a child or teenager answers in the majority language, there is still a tremendous amount to be won by persevering with the minority language, at least at home. Regularly being addressed in the minority language will often be enough to ensure that the young person has a passive command of the language. This can be turned relatively easily into an active command when required, for example when there is a communicative need for it, such as on a visit to a country where the minority language is spoken. If the language is not a part of the family's daily life, the children's knowledge of it will be difficult to maintain.

It may not always be possible to carry on using the minority language, especially if it has been actively rejected by the children. In some cases parents may find that the pressure from the majority language is too great and go over entirely to using the majority language in the family. In families where the minority language is a school language the loss might not feel too great – the young people will at least be able to keep up the language through school. In other cases the loss might be total and the youngsters might be cutting themselves off from a part of their background which they will come to miss:

> Their mother tongue for both of them now is Castilian Spanish. Both speak fluent Galician depending on the social situation they are in. If they are with their grandmother or with their friends they will speak Galician. With their mother they speak Spanish. With me now they'll usually speak Spanish. If their mother is present they'll always speak Spanish. If their mother is not present they'll unfortunately also speak Spanish. It is something I feel guilty about. I think a lot of people who grew up linguistically out of their own thing do have this guilt feeling. Should I have insisted? It was so much easier to go along with speaking Spanish and not speak English as much as I should have. I should perhaps have spoken more in English to them. Their English could have been perfect. But it's something you never know. It is easier, you know the situation. If my kids are bilingual, it is Spanish and Galician. English is very much a third language for them. Although my son is now speaking quite good Portuguese – he has been working there a lot. My daughter is learning French, German and Portuguese.
>
> (David, Galicia)

Identity

The language that people choose to use can be an expression of where they stand. Teenagers who have grown up with a minority language can easily mark their independence from their parents and their rejection of parental values by choosing not to speak the minority language. There is a good deal said about the difficulties faced by young people who grow up with two cultures. In some cases they may be left feeling like outsiders in both the majority and the minority cultures. The first aim is generally to ensure that they feel like full members of the majority culture in which they live. A secondary aim is to enable them to feel at home in the country where one or both their parents are from. If there is a subculture made up of youngsters from similar immigrant backgrounds, that may be where these young people feel most at home. The opposite can also be true and a young person can yearn to make up for lost time by learning a language they did not accept as young children:

> But at this particular time the situation at home was not really good, and two years later my parents got divorced. I had a teenage rebellion time where I backed away from my father and began to identify myself with my mother and the Turkish culture and the identity, which was hindered by not being able to speak the language. I made friends with many Turkish and Syrian people. I started to pick up the language on my own. ... What I remember is, whenever I had the possibility, I spoke Turkish. At the same time it felt slightly silly: I knew some Turkish friends, and I knew how to say, 'Hey, how are you, what are you doing?' to them. But even if I didn't know what they would answer, I would still ask these questions. So I was forcing my way through, no matter what, took every opportunity. This was easier with friends, as I was more relaxed with them compared to my relatives.
>
> (Benjamin, who grew up in Sweden)

Children of mixed parentage are often described as being half this and half that. This is a very negative way of looking at their dual linguistic and cultural affiliation. We have taught our children to think of themselves as both Swedish and Irish. Their Irishness must not be allowed to detract from their Swedishness (or vice versa). One problem with this is that they are sometimes called upon to represent Ireland – at the international school, for example, they are referred to as the Irish children. This is quite a burden to bear considering the limited amount of time they have spent there.

Teenagers are often concerned with finding their place in life. Being brought up in two cultures might give them a bit more to think about. The image of the young person with full linguistic and cultural competence in two languages with their associated cultures is not usually attainable in reality. However, if the teenager has active or passive skills in the minority language, perhaps steps can be taken to fill in the cultural gaps left in the minority culture by a childhood in another country. Many teenagers, even without a bilingual upbringing, spend a term or a year in a school or college abroad. This could be an excellent way for young people from a mixed or immigrant family to become more familiar with the culture associated with their second language and to bring their language skills up to scratch.

Some teenagers may feel that they need to choose between their two cultural allegiances. They need to know where they 'belong'. They might orient themselves aggressively towards the majority language/culture in the country where they live, or they might feel a strong affiliation with the minority language and culture, and go on to study that language more and maybe live in the country. Others can happily accept that they have two parallel backgrounds, cultures and languages. The problem then is deciding which side to support in international sports competitions!

Advice from other parents

Parents raising children with two languages in many countries were asked what advice they would give to those starting out. Their answers are often contradictory and reflect each individual family's situation and experience. No one solution will work for everyone. Take what you can use from the advice offered!

> It's a little like feeding a child; offer a rich assortment of experiences, books, tapes, friends, acquaintances, travel, stay with relatives, anything. But do not force-feed.
>
> (Thomas Beyer, USA)

1   Parents should use their native language(s) to the child, rather than deliberately trying to teach the child a particular language. They should realise that the child will pick up the community language without being taught it.

2   Parents in such situations should demand bilingual education as a right. If the minority language is too much of a minority for this to be feasible, it will need special effort to keep it up. If it is only used in the home, the child will never develop fully fledged skills, including literacy in the language.

3   Keep a diary of the child's language, noting striking usages such as mixing and transfer. It will be a source of great amusement later, and be invaluable for diagnosis if problems should develop.

4   It is probably significant that our son's best friend at school is a bilingual Eurasian girl. Without such company he could easily feel like an outsider among monolingual Cantonese children.

(Steve Matthews, Hong Kong)

Be strict about establishing the non-community language as the language of the home. Do not switch languages. If one parent is not proficient in the foreign language it is best for that parent to stick to his/her native language. Provide opportunities for the child to hear the non-community language, by, for example, getting a weekly play-group together with other mothers/fathers and children who speak the language you are trying to teach your child. Children's TV programmes in the language can be good; although TV is a passive medium, the kids can pick new vocabulary up. Read, read, read, every night as a bedtime routine. Being in a foreign culture, exposure to that culture is automatic. This is not a problem. It is important not to lead the children into thinking that one culture is superior to another in your effort to teach your language and culture. A balance must be kept in order for that child to be happy and to be able to fit into the foreign culture. Children who are raised with a healthy attitude to both cultures and learn to appreciate cultural diversity will not have major problems making friends and fitting in. However, there is no doubt that they tend toward those who speak their home language. My girls love to be with their English-speaking friends.

(Margo Arango, Colombia)

Share your culture with your children's school by teaching a lesson about the culture, traditions, and share some food. The children come to respect and understand others. When children start school they are influenced by the school culture a great deal. As a parent you must be a part of that culture to have an influence. We expose our children to a wide variety of cultures, languages, through fairs, friends and travelling. Teach your children about both cultures and languages. Take them to visit their relatives back home. Let them know how important it is to you. Tell them stories about when you were young.

(Mother in North Carolina)

I think the children have to be placed in situations where they have no choice but to communicate in the minority language.

(Sean Golden, Barcelona)

Try to balance the exposures to the languages the children are learning. The less balanced the languages are outside the home, the more the home environment needs to counter the imbalance by concentrating on the less frequently used language. Don't switch back and forth. If presented with language mixing in a conversation, or, worse yet, in individual utterances (we've seen this), children will pick one language and stick with it. Expose them maximally to both, at all levels. The ideal is to be able to have parallel tracks, so that everything experienced in one language and culture is also experienced in the other. This is obviously impossible for all situations, but the closer you can come, the better.

(Charles Hoequist, USA)

I used to recite nursery rhymes and fairy tales to the children, in English, when they were young. My sister sent me some tape recordings of children's songs, sung in English, that I played as background music while the children were playing. They mimicked the songs, which meant they were acquiring English phonemes. I think that this kind of 'passive' reinforcement can be very useful. It was just there in the background with no coercion or demand that they do anything about it. I did the same with Irish songs and they also mimicked the Irish.

(Sean Golden, Barcelona)

1   Total consistency in all situations (one can always explain and translate).

2   Insistence that the child uses the minority language; this creates a need similar to not being understood, and removes any choice, as is normal in monolingual acquisition anyway.

3   Creating a rich language environment through play, books, videos, songs, as many other interactants as possible (but that is often hard to achieve).

4   Being positive about the linguistic progress the child makes (however minimal), and giving the child a positive feeling about her bilinguality (treats that only happen to children who speak German because they are part of the German culture, positive arguments for being bilingual, what is better, 'one piece of chocolate or two?', modelling reactions to negative feedback from peers when the situation occurs).

(Susanne Döpke, Australia)

In the years since the first edition of this book came out I have received a large number of e-mails and letters asking for advice on how to best support children who are growing up with two languages. The following 10 tips sum up my position:

1   Talk to your children. This might seem obvious, but the more communicative parents are with their children, the richer the linguistic environment.
2   Use your own language unless there are compelling reasons why you don't want to.
3   Network! Help the children meet other children with the same languages, ideally monolingual children. You yourself can talk to other parents in the same situation, in real life or online.
4   Learn each other's language, at least a bit. I have had contact with many families who eventually give up on a minority language because one of the parents feels too left out.
5   Get or make supplementary material like age-appropriate books, DVDs, etc. Most families will not have much support for minority languages from school and the community. Parents and extended family need to put effort into providing a rich linguistic environment in the minority language.
6   Find fun things to do in the minority language.
7   Go to a country where the minority language is spoken. Leave majority language speakers at home on shorter visits.
8   Older children need more if they are to continue developing proficiency in more than one language – get it for them!
9   Keep in regular contact with family. In this age of instant communication it is cheap and easy to stay in touch online. Family are a great source of linguistic support.
10   Don't give up! Understand how children learn languages, with mixing, periodic preference for one language or the other, etc. This is not dangerous and it does not mean that the child is not capable of learning more than one language. But if you feel that your child's linguistic development is not progressing normally, do consult a professional.

Some parents choose not to speak their language to their children for various reasons. Others make an attempt to use their language with their children but abandon the venture after a period due to various pressures from the children, their partner or the world outside the family; or they never really get started. Nonetheless, children in every country are growing up with two languages which are not both spoken by their peers. They have vastly different family situations and the languages involved include most of the languages of the world. When they become adults, some of these children will be indistinguishable from their monolingual peers in both languages; others will have less than native mastery of one of the languages.

Chapter 10

Looking back on a bilingual childhood

Grown-up children

Depending on the circumstances of their childhood, people who grew up with two languages will have varying levels of proficiency in their two languages. Some may be native-like in both languages. Others may have one strong language and less knowledge of the other. People who grew up with a passive knowledge of a minority language may find that a visit to the country where the language is spoken can push them to be active speakers. They may find that they know much more of the language than they thought. It is possible for them as adults to improve their language skills.

A person with very little knowledge of one of the languages she heard growing up may want to learn the language as an adult. In some cases such adult learners might find that they can learn to speak the minority language easily and with good pronunciation. All that is needed is an opportunity to develop proficiency and to actually use the language.

Those who were active speakers of both languages throughout childhood and adolescence may be able to use their languages regularly at work or in their spare time. It is easy to let one of the languages fall into disuse if opportunities to use it are not sought out. An account of some of the research into the processes behind the loss of a language is given in Chapter 11.

The next generation

When those who grew up with two languages themselves become parents they may or may not choose to pass on both their languages. This decision will depend partly on the young family's linguistic situation. Are both parents proficient in both languages? Where do they live? Does the parent who grew up with two languages feel confident in his or her ability to be a good language model?

There may be pressure from the minority language-speaking grandparent (or grandparents) to pass on the second language. A grandmother who has devoted years to helping her son or daughter become a competent speaker of her native language may be disappointed if she cannot communicate with her grandchildren in the same language. In some situations the answer may be to involve the minority language-speaking grandparent in the linguistic upbringing of the child. If they meet often enough (at least several times a week from the child's first year) the grandmother may be able to establish her native language with the child.

If the other parent does not speak or even understand the minority language, it might be difficult to arrange this kind of system. In such circumstances the aim of giving a grandchild a second language from childhood is probably not worth the friction it might cause in the young family.

Cases

The following 10 cases are descriptions of childhoods contributed in interviews with adults who have themselves grown up with more than one language. Looking back on one's childhood it is possible to see patterns and decisions differently from when in the middle of events. While there are similarities between the stories, each case is unique. Some of the people interviewed here have children of their own, and they tell of the choices they have made for their children in the light of their own background. Excerpts from some of these interviews can be found on the companion website.

Case 1: Catalan and Castilian in Spain in the 1960s and 1970s

Pilar (not her real name) grew up in the countryside in the border area of La Franja in Catalonia with her three sisters. She was raised speaking Catalan to her mother and Castilian Spanish to her father, who moved with his family from southern Spain at the age of 18. The girls spoke Spanish together, and while Pilar was aware that this made them different from their friends, it proved impossible to change the system they had established:

> Yes, actually I tried once to speak Catalan with my youngest sister. We decided to try to speak Catalan among ourselves because

Catalan was the language mostly spoken at school. We noticed a difference, and we didn't want to stand out. So we said we were going to speak Catalan, but we lasted two minutes, because it didn't feel as if I was talking to my sister. The sense of strangeness was huge, I guess.

Pilar is satisfied with her upbringing with two languages, clearly separated with the one person–one language method. She returns to the strong association she has between the language chosen and the relationship between speakers:

I think it was quite balanced because my mum always used Catalan and my dad refused to use Catalan, so there was no confusion. But he did understand Catalan. So it's not like he was left out. We would speak Spanish, but as kids we felt the difference, living in a village, where most people spoke Catalan. I didn't normally mind, and it just didn't come out, speaking Catalan with my dad. Because it wouldn't be my dad if we spoke Catalan.

The Catalan spoken in La Franja is influenced by Spanish. Pilar thinks this has increased language mixing in this widely bilingual population:

Well, apart from the phonetics, which are quite different [from standard Catalan], for the vocabulary I felt that there was a strong influence of Spanish into the Catalan that was spoken in the play-ground. ... In Catalan it is very easy to have influence from Spanish to Catalan and Catalan to Spanish, especially in the area where I come from. I remember learning some words I would never use, like the Catalan word for carpet, which has nothing to do with the Spanish one. ... Like in the playground, no one would use the Catalan word for carpet, everybody would use a Catalanised version of the Spanish word. ... But that would be called a bar-barism. We wouldn't drift between languages. It wouldn't be acceptable to put a Spanish word into Catalan.

Because of her mixed family background she feels more proficient in Spanish than some of her classmates and now, living outside Spain, Catalan is not the only language she uses:

They say it makes it easier to learn other languages if you are bilingual. I don't know to what extent it is true, but I think you have more resources. I have noticed that when learning Italian, for example. And I haven't studied French, but I can read French if it's not very specialised text. [I speak] Spanish and Catalan, of course, English, Swedish, Italian and German. ... Sometimes I think of a word in English instead of Catalan.

Case 2: Igbo, Nigerian Pidgin English, English and Yoruba in Nigeria in the 1980s and 1990s

Grace (not her real name) grew up in the eastern part of Nigeria in a village with her grandparents, while her parents were working in Lagos. Igbo was the only language she spoke until she went to school and encountered Nigerian Pidgin English:

> At that age, when I was young, Igbo was the only language I knew – that was my language. Although English was the official language of Nigeria, there was no opportunity to speak that. ... The funny thing was that they weren't speaking English in the primary school. In Nigeria we have this broken language, we call it Pidgin English, so I had to learn that language and that was a kind of disadvantage for me. Usually I was supposed to have learned English, but because of the environment that I was living in, I had to learn that broken language.

At the age of 12, Grace went to school in Lagos, and she was at a disadvantage as she spoke Nigerian Pidgin English but not English. At that time, Grace and her mother spoke several languages together. Her mother was keen that she learn to speak English, not Nigerian Pidgin English, which she refers to as 'Broken':

> My mother would speak Broken, sometimes English, sometimes Igbo. ... Some parents would not mind if their children spoke Pidgin or spoke correct English. It doesn't matter for them. But this was very important for me, because as you grow up you tend to want to fit into your environment properly. Everyone around me was speaking English, so I wanted to speak that language.

In Lagos, Grace came to speak Yoruba too:

> I didn't study Yoruba, but in the environment in which I lived in Lagos, people around me spoke Yoruba and Pidgin English, so I had to also learn that one. If I didn't learn Yoruba it would be a problem for me because they would use this to abuse me. It was very important that I knew how to speak the language at the age of 12.

Igbo was no longer a priority for her in Lagos:

> I had to limit my speaking Igbo because I needed to learn this English at all costs, because my classmates didn't understand me. It was a problem for me. I was really shy at first because I didn't understand what people were saying around me. We were from different parts of Nigeria. Some spoke Hausa, some spoke Yoruba, some spoke Igbo and some spoke Idoma and the other languages.

The need to fit in linguistically has stayed with Grace:

> At a particular point in time, I had to move to a particular part of Nigeria, Delta State, and the kind of Igbo that is spoken in that environment was different from my own Igbo. So I picked from that language too. I was 21, so that also affected me in a different way because when I speak Igbo I don't speak the way I spoke when I was a young girl.

She has some advice for parents of young children who are in a situation where there are several languages around:

> I think my advice for all parents should be that every parent should endeavour to teach their children their first language. It is very important that they are able to speak their language. Because this is a huge problem when a child cannot speak his own language, when he meets the people of his language he is not able to do anything. English is important, it is a global language, but it is not enough. You have to try and teach your child the native language. It is very important.

Her feelings about English are mixed:

> It would have been interesting if I had grown up with English. I think that would have helped me a lot. I would have been able to speak better than I do.

Nonetheless, Grace is critical of parents in Nigeria who choose to bring up their children as English speakers:

> There are parents in Nigeria who do not speak their language to their children. When you speak to them you end up making a fool

of yourself because they don't understand. … If I have children in the future I am going to start by speaking my language, Igbo, with them. That is very important. They need to be able to interact with people. They need to mix with people of their own culture.

Case 3: Latvian and Russian in Latvia in the 1950s

Larisa grew up in Riga, speaking Russian with her Russian father and bilingual Latvian-Russian mother:

> As a little child I was totally unaware, because my babysitter was Latvian, my grandfather was Latvian and I spent all summers with him and with Latvian relatives, and the nursery school was in Latvian. But because of their ambitions, my parents thought that, well, a provincial education, it is better to send a single child to a Russian school because that will give access to, well, maybe better universities.
>
> At the beginning of my life there was more Latvian than Russian because of the nursery school, and babysitters and the summers. That was post-war Latvia, in Riga. My father was Russian, and my maternal grandmother was also Russian, so mum was half Latvian. My father was totally Russian and he never learned Latvian properly. He was a scientist and felt it was better to spend the time with English. Mum was totally bilingual and her Latvian grandfather, he had very poor knowledge of Russian. She spoke both languages but she preferred Russian. The dominance was Russian. She spoke Latvian when we had Latvian relatives around. The circle of relatives and playmates were Latvian, at nursery school, and we were in Latvia.

When Larisa started school, she was faced with having Russian all around her:

> I didn't realise that I most probably spoke with an accent when I started first class, and children commented. … I became aware I was a bilingual child, but before school it was totally normal. I never wondered which language to use. When you have a Latvian cousin you talk Latvian; when you have a Russian guest you talk Russian. It never occurred to me.

When she went to university at the age of 21, it was in Moscow, and her accent still caused her problems:

My Russian professor, head of the department of general linguistics, found my Russian sounded a bit Jewish. He hated it. Now I wonder if it was because I went to the Russian school that was full of Jewish kids. We grew up for 11 years together. I mixed with those people. They all came from middle-class families and they were my classmates. I had very little contact with real Russians. And he found this provincial, Jewish flavour in my speech. He didn't like it – he commented on it and he wanted me to get rid of it. I was totally unaware of it.

Now an academic linguist and professional translator, Larisa feels that her upbringing has been a resource:

I find it natural to know several languages. My father, who was a Russian, found it difficult to have several languages, difficult to think. I was used to thinking in two languages, when I was a child, but now I don't. I don't think in Latvian.

But in a situation such as that of post-Soviet Latvia, language and identity are closely related:

When I came back from Moscow, as a dynamic person working for the University of Latvia, that was a time for national re-reckoning. Quite a number of my friends who were intellectual dissidents were involved in this movement. They were Latvian nationalists. And they questioned my political identity in this situation, the Latvian intellectuals. Then I suffered that I was not sent to the Latvian school to become a 100 per cent Latvian intellectual. That was an inspiring time. I couldn't belong – because I became too Russianised because of my life in Moscow and belonging also to a group of Russian intellectuals who were quite amazing people. I had problems of a split personality as a linguist. That was a time when I really felt sorry about the choice of my parents. I didn't feel Latvian in a situation where I would love to be. When you are mixed you are divided in a way, in particular when it is politically an acute moment. You really don't know which side you belong to because you have both sides in you.

After a long period outside Latvia, in Russia and in Sweden, she had to pass an exam to qualify for Latvian citizenship:

Latvia became independent and I lost my Latvian citizenship because I wasn't of pure Latvian heritage. It was a tough time for mixed people. I had to restore my Latvian citizenship by going through a state language exam. And the examiners were surprised at my accent; they said my accent was like a Latvian immigrant. I had been living for 10 years in Sweden at that time, or less, maybe six. So they reacted. They thought I sounded native. We have many second generation immigrants to Canada, Sweden, and I sounded more like them, and they thought maybe I had a Latvian background from a family of immigrants but I didn't sound like a Latvian who grew up in Soviet Latvia. Maybe it has to do with interference from Swedish. ... They really couldn't identify me from my language. There was Latvian, there was something that was not exactly Latvian.

Case 4: Scots and English in Scotland in the 1960s

David grew up in Scotland, speaking Scots and English. He soon became aware that the choice of Scots or English was sensitive:

> I became aware of Scots at a very young age, thanks to a school-teacher at my school in Edinburgh who was very keen on the Scots language. ... I was very interested because my grandparents used many parts of Scots, and I remember some words I used at home, and at school I was told not to use them, that they were Scots, they weren't proper English. So when I discovered Burns, at the age of about 10, I became very interested in the Scots language in the way that only a 10-year-old can. ... So the Scots language was something very romantic to me. It was associated with Burns, and it was also associated with naughtiness. If I use Scots words at school I'll get told off. I was told off for speaking Scots at home too. I remember being told by a member of my family, 'Dinnae say dinnae. It's no proper English.'

David sees parallels in this with his wife's background with Castilian Spanish and Galician in La Coruña in Galicia in northwestern Spain, where he now lives with his family:

> Her parents were native Galician speakers. They spoke Galician to each other and to their daughter all the time. But my wife was encouraged by her parents and by the social milieu to speak Castilian Spanish. That was a way of getting away from the village, away from the peasant stock that was her lot. She was given a scholarship to a convent school which was a part of social

movement. So she was encouraged by her parents to speak back to them in Castilian Spanish. My wife understands Galician perfectly; she would be able to speak it if she tried. She doesn't try although she agrees politically with the importance of the Galician language.

Before going to Galicia, David was offered a job teaching English in Catalonia:

> Now if it had been anywhere else I wouldn't have been interested, but I was involved politically quite heavily as a student, as most of us were. Catalonia rang a lot of bells and pressed a lot of buttons, as it were. I had been following the post-Franco era with the wildcat strikes in the socialist press of the UK, so I was interested in Catalonia. I was also interested in the linguistic aspect of Catalonia. I knew they had their own language and I knew this was trying to be reclaimed after it had been oppressed by Francoism. This was also a time when as part of my political development I was becoming aware that as a Scot living in England at the time I was also denied access to language or languages that could have been what I thought was my political birthright.

He also chose to go to Galicia for political reasons:

> I'd heard of the Basque Country, and followed the struggles in the Basque Country; I'd heard of the linguistic situation in Catalonia, but Galicia was totally new to me. So I decided to hitchhike over to Galicia, not being quite sure how far it was from Catalonia. I thought, if I ever get a chance of a job there, I'll take it. Well I got a chance of a job there and I met the woman who was to become my wife, and that's how I got to Galicia.

When he was 14, David moved with his family to Newark in England. This meant that he had to adapt to a new set of linguistic norms and realised that the English he spoke was not widely understood:

> I remember the first class I went to was geography. I could not understand a word the guy said, not a word. He was speaking ordinary English. The kids obviously took the piss out of me rotten for my accent. I had a broad Edinburgh accent, much stronger than my accent is now. I believe I still have something of a Scottish accent; then I had a very strong working class Edinburgh accent.

Even if I wasn't using Scots words and phrases like *dinnae* and *ken*, and that, which I wasn't, I was trying as best I could to speak as standard English as possible, but I was using words like *scunner* and that, but just the breadth of my accent made my speech inaccessible to most of the people around me and their accents were inaccessible to me. This is something that when you are 14 marks you, but also it changes in no time, and in a couple of weeks you're trying to copy their accent. I always had this wee bit of resentment, I must admit.

So now, in Galicia, David has encouraged his children to speak Galician even though his wife's use of the language is receptive only:

It's common in fact in Galicia, it's like a lost generation. There should be some studies made of it because my wife's case is not unique. ... Of course the prestige of the Galician language within certain circles has changed. Galician is losing speakers in its heartland, the country areas where it's still seen as unprestigious, and Castilian is encouraged by the press, by the television, by translations of video games and this kind of thing. In the cities, people who are going to universities and studying are seeing Galician for the first time as being a prestigious language. It's almost like a badge saying that you are left wing or that you are progressive or socially aware. It's saying that you are not a fascist. Speaking Galician is very much a statement of who I am among young Galician people.

Case 5: Italian and English in England in the 1950s and 1960s

Loretta grew up in London with an Italian mother and an English Jewish father and an older sister and brother. Her mother spoke both 'bad English', as Loretta says, and Italian with her when she was young:

What I can remember of my early childhood is that my mother couldn't speak English properly, but of course she could speak Italian. So I was probably brought up with a mix of Italian and bad English from my mother's side, but it didn't seem to affect my learning of the English language. I spoke in my early years better Italian than English from home, but I started school when I was four so therefore my English developed as anybody else's English developed.

Loretta's sister spoke better Italian than she did, though with a stronger English accent, as her mother, being homesick, wanted to spend time in Italy. This went on through Loretta's childhood:

> I remember playing in the garden with my cousins and their friends. We were all reasonably the same age and somebody began darting all these questions at me. What should I do? ... Sometimes I said yes and they looked at me very surprised. I probably didn't get one answer right, but I thought, better that than to say I didn't understand the question.

Later Loretta's Italian improved, as the result of more summers in Italy and continuing to speak Italian with her mother. She remembers when she began to feel proficient in Italian:

> I was around 12 or 13 years old. We went to Italy for three months. I was playing in the village with my cousins and I was one of the gang. I understood them and they understood me, and at some point they said, 'Loretta, you really speak good Italian.' Then I realised that not only did I speak good Italian, but my sister who speaks very, very good Italian retains to this day an English accent, and my Italian was more Italian. That's probably in my eardrums somewhere that I have a better ear, or that I spent more time with my mother at an earlier age, I don't know. But I always spoke better Italian than my brother and sister.

Loretta's mother and her language were a source of great pride and great embarrassment to her as she grew up:

> My mother always encouraged the Italian language within the family, and the Italian culture. I was ashamed of it as a teenager. Of the Italian, of the loudness, of the passionate nature. If I invited a boyfriend home it would always have to be on a Friday evening because Friday evening was family evening and everybody had to meet this boyfriend, and then he would come out of the dinner shell-shocked. Most of them thought it was fantastic – oh, what a wonderful family. So the shame turned into, well, maybe this is quite fun to be half Italian then. Then I became more interested in the language and proud of knowing the language instead of, well, I can speak it but don't spread the word. ... Also, my mother, when she walked into a room everyone knew. So even the behaviour wasn't typically English. On parents' days, mums and dads would

come in normally dressed. My mum would come in as the most elegant one – back straight, walking in with what would be perceived as her slightly arrogant look, which it wasn't, it was just the way it was.

Of course this family history has influenced Loretta's choices when bringing up her own children with her Swedish husband in Sweden:

[I raised them] in English. You have to choose a language. I tried to be as consistent as possible. I have never spoken Swedish with my husband. Many people are surprised at that. Some of my friends in this situation woke up one morning and said, 'Right, we're going to speak Swedish from now on.' I didn't see the point because my husband spoke absolutely perfect English. We didn't have a problem communicating in English. When he communicates with the children it's in Swedish. When we are sitting as a family it is bilingual. I will speak English, and never move from English, except for Swedish words that come in, one word here and one word there, but I just keep to English all the time. I am comfortable with it and all my kids are as well. They can move from Swedish to English without a problem. It's everyday fare for us. Now they are getting boyfriends and girlfriends, so last weekend my son came home with his girlfriend and we were sitting at the table and it was bilingual still even though she was sitting there. English is a language that she'll understand well, so we didn't feel we were alienating her in any way. Eventually, I was speaking to her in English too and she was answering me in English so it was all very familiar for everyone. That's one of the advantages with a language like English. In England, Italian was something they'd never understand in a million years.

Loretta's children are now, as adults, very fluent in English, and interested in learning Italian. Her only regret is that her mother wasn't more consistent in speaking Italian with her. She advises parents of young children not to succumb to pressure to drop the minority language:

You have to encourage a multilingual world, and the place to start is in your family if you have two or three languages in the family. … But it's tough and they're going to hate you for it sometimes and they're going to be embarrassed and refuse to answer you in your language. They're going to do all these horrible things, but you just have to keep going. When the day comes that they realise all the positive things that you can get from knowing another language they will love you for it and thank you.

Case 6: Farsi, Czech and English in Scotland in the 1980s

Adam (not his real name) grew up with three languages in constant use. English was the majority language in Scotland, where he lived with his Czech Dad, Iranian mum and his brother. Adam's father was determined that his sons should learn his language:

> I think it was my father who was the driving force. He insisted that each parent speak their native language to us. I think mum was a bit less draconian. Dad was quite strict on it. They insisted that communication would be in the language of the parent. If we said something in English, Dad would say the correct thing in Czech and insist that we repeat it. ... We could get away with more English with Mum. Each of them talked to us in their language, Farsi and Czech, and I think that initially, when I went to school for the first time, my English wasn't that good. My first two languages were Czech and Farsi.

Living in Scotland, as soon as Adam started school his English developed rapidly:

> Once I'd got to the age of five or six, English became at least my first language. I don't know about my brother. School and friends were all in English. Even though my English wasn't good when I started school, I didn't really experience it as a handicap. When you are a kid you pick these things up really well.

He found his father's determination trying at times when he was young:

> There were times when I didn't like it – I got annoyed. At times he would do Czech dictation or he was teaching me to tell the time in Czech. I remember one episode quite vividly. He was taking a bit of time to teach me, and my friends were outside playing football. He would insist on me and my brother repeating things [in Czech] if we said it in English. Now, looking back on it, yes, it might have been annoying at times, but I am now very grateful for the skill of having Czech. It has proved immensely

useful at times. If I didn't have it there would be a whole tradition or culture that I would be separated from. I have quite a few friends in Czech; we have a house there. I can't imagine not having that now and it is important to me.

Adam's mother was more easygoing, which meant that he did not always speak Farsi with her:

Between the ages of 12 and my teenage years my Farsi was initially quite good and then I got quite lazy and didn't make the effort and we'd speak to my mum in English more than half the time. But after I finished school, actually I spent part of my gap year in Iran; when I came back I made a conscious effort to speak more Farsi with my mum, so now it's up to about 80 per cent. My Farsi is domestic. I'm fluent in things around the house.

The family moved to France for a while, and Adam spent two years in a French school between the ages of 15 and 17:

My parents insisted, and I would agree with them, that I go to a French school and just start off where I left off in Scotland. So I went to a local French lycée and yes, at first that was pretty daunting, and quite hard. I struggled for the first term, I'd say, but it came really quickly. By the end of the second year I did my bac and I passed.

Adam is also fluent in German, the result of a school year spent on his own in Germany:

That was in second year, at the age of 13. I went to Germany to learn German for a year. I stayed with a local family we found. ... I had no German whatsoever. I was pretty much a beginner. I came back [to Scotland] in third year and picked up where I left off.

The only problem this remarkable young man has with his language situation is that he tries to avoid calling attention to his skills:

I think sometimes I felt more embarrassed in my ability. I could do all this and others couldn't. I felt that by being able to do that I was showing off. So I tried not to bring attention to it too much. I'd be quite quiet about it, probably still am. I don't say, 'Hey, look at me. I can speak however many languages.' Sometimes I am embarrassed to admit, okay, I speak all these languages, but more from an embarrassment than that it makes me possibly look bigheaded.

His advice to parents in the position his own parents were in is clear:

> I'd say definitely go for teaching your kids your own languages. I think it's one of the best things my parents did for me, after having me, I suppose. Some people say, 'Oh, they'll pick up the languages later, or they won't integrate into their local surroundings, whatever language that is, the culture.' But at that age, when kids start mixing with other kids it's not an issue, they pick up things so quickly. Little kids are sponges. The more you can teach them at an early age, the better. You gain so much from it: culture, tradition, this ability to talk with that many more people and exchange ideas.

Adam believes that language is the foundation of thought, which, he argues, makes it a good thing to know many languages:

> I suppose there is a school of thought that says you are limited in your thought by your language so you can only think as far as you can describe what you are thinking. So if you have more languages there are more holes that are plugged. There are more specific terms for ideas or concepts or whatever. I think that can only be good. I know there are certain terms that I think of, like the word for me is the word in Farsi or in Czech because it fits just right. That's the word for that thing. The English equivalent is just not adequate.

Like others whose experiences are described here, Adam is aware that the decision to raise your children with more than one language can be controversial in some settings, but he believes that it is worth persevering:

> I would say just go for it; no matter what other people around you say, stick with the languages.

Case 7: Swedish and Danish in Sweden in the 1950s

Pia (not her real name) was born in Stockholm to Danish parents:

> They have always spoken Danish together and to us, myself and my brother. I must have spoken Danish until I started playing with

other children. I asked my mother, she's 91, when I started speaking Swedish. She said around three, when I started being outside.

I still speak Danish to my mother and I have quite a few cousins. I go there every summer and of course Danish is our language. My Swedish is better, I would say. My oral proficiency in Danish, if I have been to Denmark for a week or two, I feel it is coming back. But with my mother I realise we use some Swedish words as well, when there is a better Swedish word.

Pia was aware that she had two languages when she started school:

I read books in Danish and in Swedish. No problem reading but when we had dictation in school there were some mix-ups. My spelling was not that good at the beginning – I had to think. Also I know that my written proficiency is not as good in Danish. I write letters and things, but I know I make spelling mistakes.

Danish and Swedish are closely related to each other. Pia sees this as both an advantage and a disadvantage:

I think that's why I mixed some, especially with the spelling. Also you know you can make yourself understood, even if you speak the other language. People can say to my mother, it's very easy to understand when you speak Danish, but actually she believes she is speaking Swedish. That's a bit sad. I feel now that she is getting older she doesn't really realise. Also because my husband is there so there's a mixture of languages all the time. I turn to my mother and speak Danish; to my husband I speak Swedish. We all seem to understand each other. I think it is more difficult when the languages are so close. You don't have to learn.

Pia believes that her parents made a good choice in consistently speaking Danish to their children:

They were very consistent. They had good friends who came to Sweden at the same time and started working together, but they had the idea that they should try to speak Swedish to their children. That was a terrible mixture of languages. They didn't speak Swedish and they didn't speak Danish. I still think that their language is not Swedish and not Danish. I think my parents made a good choice.

She spoke Danish with her brother until he moved to Florida at the age of 25:

Then he started speaking English of course. Now he has moved back to Sweden, and we speak Swedish together. He manages to speak Danish to my mother but for us it seems more natural now to speak Swedish.

Pia remembers code switching when young, but she is now in the reversed position of trying to help her elderly mother from losing her Danish altogether:

I think I used words, vocabulary; when I found better words in Swedish I would just exchange the Danish word for the Swedish one. Now I say to my mother, we have to keep to the Danish, when she forgets. I think it is important for her too to keep that.

Pia spoke only Swedish with her own children, but they had a lot of contact with her mother when they were growing up and all understand Danish and will try a bit to speak it. Her advice for parents is:

I think it is very positive to have two languages, even if I think that my Swedish developed, especially written proficiency developed slower. Also I realise that when I started school, for example the name of flowers, tools, the kitchen things, the things we only spoke about in the family, I didn't know the names in Swedish.

She believes that her early exposure to two languages may have helped her pronounce further learned languages better:

I remember learning German at school and they said, 'Well, your pronunciation is excellent.' I think some of the sounds there were helped by having Danish as well. Probably having more sounds in your mouth made it easier to imitate.

Case 8: Hindko, Pashto, Punjabi, English and Urdu in Pakistan in the 1980s and 1990s

Nazir grew up in Lahore in southern Pakistan with parents from Mansehra in the north. His parents were Hindko speakers and the family lived in a neighbourhood with other northerners who spoke Pashto:

My parents came from the north, where the major languages were Pashto and Hindko. In the home my parents spoke Hindko to each other, and Pashto to us children. We listened and in time we understood this language well. Many Pashto speakers came to the city. They were friends of my parents and spoke Pashto, not Hindko. They came and lived together in the same street. So their children spoke good Pashto and I was used to playing with them. These two languages were common, especially Pashto in my childhood.

When Nazir started school his language situation became more complex:

> After the age of four or five I went to school and in school it was our national language, which is Urdu. It was compulsory to speak only Urdu in the school, eight or nine hours a day. The common language of the south province was Punjabi. Punjabi was very common, not in the offices or schools, but outside, in the common life. So outside, in the market and the shops or visiting, the language was Punjabi, the language of that province, Punjab. I was also used to speaking this, not in my early years, but from eight to 10 years when I was out with other children I would speak Punjabi. These four languages were very common in my life. I always used to speak Pashto at home and outside the home.

Nazir did not find it difficult to communicate in Urdu and Punjabi, and believes that watching TV helped him before he started school:

> We looked at TV, at series and cartoons, all in Urdu. There were only one or two programmes in Punjabi. Otherwise everything was in Urdu or English. So it also helped us to understand Urdu from the beginning. You know, Punjabi and Urdu, there is not so much difference. And I think from television I learned more Urdu. We always used to see television. They only used to speak Urdu. Yes, there was a little problem in the beginning, but I didn't find any problem to speak with my friends. I don't remember that it was a problem to speak Urdu.

In addition, English was introduced early in Nazir's schooling:

> When I started school at four and a half or five my parents sent me to a good school that offered English from the first level. I could understand the basics of English at that age. We learned to read and write English at the same time as in Urdu. We studied maths in English after two or three years. This was a good step in Pakistan, where English is an official language.

The ability to use English is important in Pakistan and gives its speakers status:

> Urdu is the national language of Pakistan. You can use this language everywhere in the street, schools and offices and they will understand you are a good and educated person. In our Urdu there are many sentences in English. People use English and Urdu mixed, so then other people will think, 'Yes, he has very good manners, very good education. He knows how to treat others, how to respect others with words and sentences.' You can also speak Punjabi or Pashto. They are also good languages, but they are provincial languages, not the national language. Urdu and English are the national languages.

Nazir was aware from an early age that his parents spoke a different language to each other than to him:

> I was aware that they were speaking a different language than I had at school and that I spoke myself. But Hindko, Punjabi and Urdu, there is so little difference. Pashto is quite different. In our street there were many people living who spoke Punjabi so we learned Punjabi easily, but they never learned Pashto.

Nazir is glad he has his linguistic skills and would pass on more than one language to any child he might have in the future, but he feels the majority language is most important:

> It depends where we will be. I would prefer to speak the main language of that place. In Sweden I would speak Swedish and Pashto and English. I will try Pashto, but I don't think it will be good because no one will speak Pashto with him or her.

Case 9: Turkish and Swedish in Sweden in the 1980s

Benjamin has been living in Istanbul for the past year, but he grew up in Sweden. His mother moved from Turkey to Sweden with her parents when she was eight and his father is Swedish. Benjamin heard Turkish while growing up, but his mother did not usually speak Turkish to him:

> I grew up hearing Turkish all the time. My mother spoke it to her sister and her parents. Almost the whole family went to Sweden.

She had a brother and a sister. The thing was that my mother, by leaving Turkey at the age of eight, and not really studying it at all in Sweden and not really going back to Turkey to keep the language alive, she was left with a child's Turkish. Of course she could communicate and manage fine in Turkish, but still, the fact that her Swedish has become better than her Turkish, combined with the fact with that my father does not speak Turkish, kept her from teaching us the language. There are several other factors too, but these are the most obvious ones.

Despite this, Benjamin's mother tried to make him familiar with some Turkish:

> When I was a kid, perhaps three or four years old, she tried to teach me the vocabulary of Turkish. She used words that rhymed, so it would be easy. It is quite funny, she did a good job. Apparently I knew words such as fork, knife, plane, window, cupboard, things like these. And then, one day (I have no memory of this), an old Turkish woman approached us, and they talked. And my mother was so proud of me, because I knew these words. And she went: 'Go on, say these words.' And I gave her a couple of examples. And this woman pinched my chin in a very sinister way, so I started to cry. After that day, my mother says that she could not get any Turkish out of me. I guess she tried a little bit and I didn't want to speak Turkish, because I associated it with the pain. From that point, I didn't know any Turkish. I knew words such as 'Hello', 'How are you?', and some religious terms, because we were still raised Muslim. But they are mostly Arabic.

His parents' divorce when he was 12 meant that Benjamin became more interested in his Turkish heritage:

> I had a teenage rebellion time and began to identify myself with my mother and the Turkish culture and identity, which was hindered by not being able to speak the language. I made friends with many Turkish and Syrian people. I started to pick up the language on my own. There weren't any Turkish people in the area I was living in, but when I was 13 I started in a new school more centrally located. It had Turkish students too. It was coincidental, but that is how I met these Turkish people. I really enjoyed learning Turkish this way, but it was difficult. What I remember is, whenever I had the possibility, I spoke Turkish. At the same time it felt

slightly silly. I knew some Turkish friends, and I knew how to say, 'Hey, how are you? What are you doing?' to them. But even if I didn't understand the answer, I would still ask these questions. So I was forcing my way through, no matter what, took every opportunity. This was easier with friends, as I was more relaxed with them compared to my relatives. With my mother I was not relaxed at all. It felt very forced and fake to speak Turkish with her. It didn't feel right. As she didn't speak Turkish with me, the development didn't occur at all. I visited many Turkish relatives in Stockholm, and became closer to them. With relatives, it went better, as their Turkish was a lot better than my mother's, and then I could ask, and they would explain and I made a note in my head.

Benjamin wishes things had been different when he was growing up:

My mother sent me and my brother to the mosque. They had us reading Arabic, which we didn't understand, reading the Qu'ran, and it felt ironic in some way: they send us here to read Arabic, just to learn to read it, not understand it. And at home there is a language that carries so much more, so many relevant things for us, and she didn't teach us that. I wished that my mother would have spoken the language to me. Of course, the learning experience was crucial for me as a teenager and a human being, and it also brought me here [to Istanbul], where I met my wife, so I am very grateful for that. But, this is something I have realised now: I was struggling, and I could ask my mother a thousand times: why didn't you just learn? Even though her Turkish wasn't very developed, it's just about talking, and it's just to start talking to the children, so they at least learn something. I started from zero.

Nonetheless, something of Benjamin's early exposure to Turkish must have stayed with him. Now, after just a year in Istanbul, Benjamin is fluent in Turkish and can sometimes pass as a native speaker:

My awareness of Turkish of course is to large extent about grammar rules and vocabulary and opposites and so forth. But pronunciation was something you could practice infinitely. It's just repetition, really. I have always had this talent to imitate. I am good at imitating Swedish accents and also some English ones. I applied that imitation talent to Turkish and, of course, it's not perfect. Sometimes I make a big effort to sound native. If I don't get too many questions I can pull it off. Normally they think I'm from the

Balkans, sort of Balkan-Turk or something. I'm quite light-skinned compared with Turkish people from the East of Turkey. Grammatically, I would say I'm very good, but of course since I have only lived here for a year, I think that the fact that gives me away is not my grammar or my pronunciation, but the choice of phrases and idioms. There are so many in Turkish, and I am not so proficient in that area, and that is what gives me away.

Benjamin married his wife, who is a teacher of Turkish as a foreign language, just a month before our interview. He is adamant that he will pass on both his languages to any future children they might have:

I think it depends on where we would raise them, if it's in Turkey or Sweden. They would have Turkish from their mother, of course, and also from society. What I would do is teach them Swedish, and, of course, I have thought about teaching them English also, but I need to do more research about how many languages they are able to learn in a young age. Nevertheless, if I could teach them Swedish, they would have a Germanic language as their mother tongue, and learning English in school would be easier for them than having Turkish as their mother tongue as it's from a completely different language family. But I will definitely teach them Swedish. What would be more difficult is that my wife would like to be a part of that, she has to learn Swedish also. But she's very good. She speaks good English and has taught English. She might confuse languages a bit in the beginning.

His advice to parents in the position his mother was in when he was growing up is clear:

Try to make an effort to teach the language to your children, because they will thank you so much, in the end. Even if you don't have the time or the will, or the linguistic knowledge required to make an effort, just talk. Just talk and pass it on as much as you can. Because it will stick, you know, and one day, even if the children don't speak at all, they will understand a lot, and the step from not speaking to speaking will be a much smaller one. So I think that would be my advice. And just remember that language is never bad, it's always positive. They have a saying here in Turkey: one language, one man. So if you know two languages you are two men, meant in a positive way. So according to Turks, I am three men now. You can communicate and broaden your mind, amazingly. You know, it carries the culture, so that would be my advice, not to neglect it.

Case 10: Krio, English and Mende in Sierra Leone in the 1980s and 1990s

Anthony lives in Sweden now, but he grew up in Sierra Leone. His parents were Mende speakers from the interior and moved back there from Freetown, the capital, while Anthony was still a child. Anthony's first language was Krio, an English-based creole:

> I grew up in the capital city, Freetown. In Freetown we have a general language that everybody can speak, Krio. We also have 16 different dialects, and everybody speaks his or her own dialect, but Krio is a general language that everybody can speak to understand each other. I was about 11 years old when I moved back to the interior with my people. Krio was not actually common there in Bo, which was the second capital city. We had a local language called Mende. I never spoke Mende before going to Bo. In Bo the Mende people live. When I went to Bo I was forced to start learning this new language, Mende.

English is the official language of Sierra Leone and is the language used in schools:

> In school, English, everything was in English. But in the last 10 years they have changed the system a bit. Now they are trying to teach people the local languages in school. So people in the capital city Freetown can choose if they want to learn Krio, or Mende or Susu or Temne, in school. When I was in Freetown, in class 3 or 4 we were talking English and Krio. In the playground Krio mostly. English was taught in school, but after school we talked our language, which was Krio. When I went to the interior, to Bo, I didn't speak Mende. I only spoke Krio, but most of my school-mates when I started school in Bo could not speak Krio properly, they only spoke Mende and a little bit of English in school. So I would go to the playground and try to speak Mende and I tried to speak Krio. So through the playground, where we used to hang out together, playing football, being with them and that is how I actually learned Mende firstly. It was not that difficult at my age, at 11 or 12; I really tried to adapt to the system as quick as possible as I was trying to learn the language. The community was only

Mende, about 98 per cent spoke Mende. You go to the shop: Mende; you go to the town: Mende; you go to a ball field its Mende. So within a year I could actually speak Mende properly. It was fast and simple for me.

Anthony's family did not share his problems as they were originally from the Mende-speaking interior:

> The adults in my home spoke Mende because they are Mende. Everybody in the house spoke Mende. I could not speak it, but most of them, like my elder sister, they have lived in Mendeland so they could speak it perfectly.

Despite this background, Anthony did not learn to speak Mende at home in Freetown:

> They tried to speak Mende to me, but not every day. They only spoke Mende at home. I spent more time with my friends speaking Krio and English. When I came home they talked Mende but mostly I didn't understand what they were saying. So I never learned to talk Mende in Freetown with my people. I only learned to talk Mende when I went to Bo, with my friends. I was determined to learn the language. I had to be with my friends and make new friends and go out and play. Even though I wasn't much interested in football I went out and played. Then I started speaking. People were somewhat surprised and happy that I learned the dialect. We started speaking Mende at home. It came easily. I could understand most of what they were saying.

Of course Anthony's accent in Mende was and still is influenced by his Krio:

> Yes, I came like a city boy to the interior. They used to call me Kriobobo, a city man. Because I was new, I didn't speak Mende. It was both negative and positive.

Later, Anthony learned other languages:

> Susu is one of the Sierra Leone languages. I really learned it when I was in Guinea. Susu is one of the major languages. I applied the same system as when I started talking Mende. Wherever I go, I want to talk the language. Like when I came to Sweden. When I

came to Guinea I tried to make phrases and to learn the local language. I was 16–17 when I started learning Susu.

English is the only language Anthony has learned to write in:

> I had English from my first day at school. Even now I am studying in English. I have been studying English as my primary language from childhood. If I write in Mende or Krio, I only write according to the sounds. Nowadays, many people who have studied it in school write perfectly in Mende or Krio. Now the teachers teach how to write these languages. When I went to school I never had the opportunity.

Anthony believes that it is very difficult for a child to learn a language other than the majority language where he is growing up and that it would not have helped him if his parents had spoken their language, Mende, to him when he was young in Freetown:

> Even if they had spoken Mende with me from childhood, Mende is only spoken in the interior. I was in the capital city, which is a Krio-speaking city. It would not have made any difference. But if I had been born in Bo I would have wished for them to speak Mende to me. But the city we were living in was Krio-speaking.

Now that he has a child of his own, he is sympathetic to her desire to communicate with him in Swedish, the majority language in Sweden where he lives with his Nigerian, Yoruba-speaking wife:

> We speak English with her, but she is always fighting with us to speak Swedish. I consider English as her first language and I never want English to depart from her. We started talking English in the house. Now she started pre-school just last year and now it is very difficult for her to speak English. I try to speak English to her and she responds in Swedish. I try to encourage her to speak English. She understands everything I say in English but she cannot respond to everything in English. She responds in Swedish. She speaks good Swedish and she thinks it is very difficult for her to speak English.

Anthony and his wife are keen for their daughter to grow up with English as her first language, but this is proving to be difficult in Sweden and she is losing proficiency in both English and Yoruba:

I really want her to be fluent in English. In the long run maybe she will want to study outside Sweden, maybe in an English-speaking country. If she speaks Swedish now and we travel home, she cannot communicate. If she speaks English perfectly she can communicate alright.

Leif 23;6, Anders 21;9, Patrik 18;0 and Lisa 16;6: Swedish and English in Sweden

At the time of writing the third edition of this text, my own children, whose language development has been described in the previous chapters, are in a position to look back on their linguistic background.

Anders compares his proficiency as a child with what he has now as an adult:

> When I was a young child, I think I was more proficient in both languages really because my vocabulary was basically smaller. There wasn't that much to keep track of and I had basically a full vocabulary in both Swedish and English. While now I feel it is more fractionalised and some fractions I know a lot better in Swedish and some a lot better in English. And some I can't really cross between them, which can cause difficulties. If I have studied something in one of the languages or read lots about it or even talked lots about it, I'll be able to express my thoughts about it a lot more efficiently and correctly because I can be more precise in what I'm saying, while if I have read in the other language about it I can only give a basic idea because the thoughts don't really translate so well. My vocabulary concerning language is more proficient in English. A lot of more informal things and dealing with authorities I am a lot more proficient in Swedish since I lived basically all my life in Swedish.

Anders attended English-medium lower and upper secondary school (ages 13–19) in Sweden and he has recently been studying English at university in Sweden:

> In some ways [having English at home] makes it easier. In some ways it makes it harder. I never had to learn the concepts before – I had them intuitively. But in other ways it makes it easier because I've had an easier time reading than most of the students, and writing because I've also had more practice in that since I've been studying in English for a long time, which makes it easier than for the average Swedish student who hasn't done that.

Now he speaks both languages on a daily basis:

> I have friends I speak Swedish to, friends I speak English to. The same thing with family: I speak English to my mother and Swedish to my father and siblings.

But he never speaks English with his siblings:

> No, I think that's got to do with growing up only speaking Swedish to them. It has become a strict rule in my head somehow.

As a student of language, Anders has set himself high standards of proficiency:

> I feel that I'm not entirely native in either language. I make mistakes in both languages. I often see myself that I have made mistakes, especially when I read through things I write and see it isn't a great grammar for this language. Certain parts of the language, I just don't have it for both languages. ... I try to make sure to read high level texts in both languages and somehow to cross the fields a bit when possible so I can have vocabulary in both languages. They are different and force me to think slightly differently, which has an effect on how I perceive the subject.

He can see both advantages and disadvantages of a bilingual childhood:

> I think if I was raised monolingually I wouldn't have the confusion in language that I have, but at the same time I feel that slight confusion is certainly worth it for all the advantages of having two languages. I would have probably been better at that one language if I had been raised monolingually but then I would have less languages, which wouldn't make up for that. I'm not perfectly native in either language. It's a big disadvantage to feel I can't express everything I want in any one language. I feel it's limiting in many ways. But at the same time it is at a cost that is definitely reasonable compared to what you receive.

Nonetheless, he would be keen to help any future children to become proficient in both his languages:

> I think I'd definitely try to get them to have two languages. I think that would be good for them. But at the same time I could

understand if they didn't want it, but it would be worth the effort. I would definitely try to get them to learn both English and Swedish.

Anders spent a semester as an exchange student at an English university and could usually pass as a native speaker of English:

> To the other exchange students; they were very confused. They saw me as Swedish although I spoke very good English to people in shops and I understood the discourse, which was more of a cultural thing that you might not learn at school. I think my English friends could tell, but only after speaking to me for a while.

Now back in Sweden he feels that his identity has parts of both sides:

> I think a big part of me is Swedish, but then there is also a big part of me who isn't. It's not even half and half. I mean, there's more than half of both. But I don't feel that I have two cultures either. I feel I lack something from both cultures. But I feel I fit in in the Swedish culture very well.

Leif has also had experience spending time on his own in English-speaking countries, working in Ireland, and studying in Scotland for a year:

> Limerick was interesting because then you couldn't rely on your Swedish; you had to rely on your English. If you didn't know the word you had to think. But it was interesting language-wise. In Scotland it was the same thing, you couldn't rely on your Swedish there. I could make myself understood and they could understand me, so that was not really a problem. They treated me as a Swede because there were other people from other countries so it wasn't really foreign in that way. In England or Ireland I would feel like a foreigner. I mean, okay, speaking English, but I would present myself as coming from Sweden more than being Irish or British.

Leif is positive about a bilingual upbringing:

> It's good to have two languages; even if it might be hard to teach simultaneously, it's good in the end for the child to have two languages.

Patrik remembers trying to make sense of the way languages were used:

> When I was younger I thought it was strange that people spoke Swedish to their mothers, and some bilingual people I knew also spoke English to their fathers, which I thought was strange also. In my world people spoke English to their mothers.

Patrik went through different stages with his languages:

> I remember I had periods when I only spoke Swedish or English. I remember a brief period when I think I was about seven when I could almost only speak Swedish. I spoke Swedish all the time until I went to Ireland in a monolingual English environment. Then my English recovered. Otherwise I think that as I got older, when I was perhaps about nine, I began to see my bilingualism as an advantage. Because I mean, I knew English well. It was a good thing to know.

Now he feels that his Swedish is stronger than his English:

> The English I get mostly from TV and reading and films and so on, while socially my Swedish is better because it's only my mother and my home language teacher I actually regularly speak English to. So I feel my Swedish is stronger. I haven't been in an English-speaking country for a long time. I do feel foreign, but at the same time I feel some kind of bond to the English-speaking world. I'm not completely foreign. I could manage. I know what to do in different situations, but that's more cultural than linguistic.

Patrik feels that having two languages has made it easier for him to learn Russian and German at school:

> I felt there are some advantages. Especially when I have learned grammar and the technical side, you can see, well, it's like this in Swedish and this in English. You can compare the differences. At the same time I haven't learned a foreign language until recently – I haven't learned English as a foreign language.

Patrik's advice for parents with young children is similar to that given by almost all the people interviewed in this chapter:

> They should just speak their language, their mother tongue, rather than trying to teach your children broken Swedish. I see it as an

advantage to be growing up with two languages and a mixed background. I think also some part of learning Swedish and English has been stories and culture. I remember my English language being stronger when I was younger. I had to catch up my Swedish childhood later, perhaps with children's programmes and stories. I think it is not just two languages but also cultures I have been brought up with. You have always something to tell, some story you heard when you were young, and you can relate to that. It is a great creative resource.

Conclusion

Interestingly, none of the people whose stories appear here regrets being exposed to more than one language while growing up, although many of them feel that this kind of language experience is not only positive. Children who grow up with more than one language certainly do not get an extra language for free, as is sometimes thought. There is effort and sacrifice involved, even though the parents and adult children who have told their stories here feel that the price is not too high, given the benefits associated with access to another language and culture. For teens and young adults, access to languages and cultures that form part of their heritage can be important for their sense of self.

Nonetheless, having more than one language can be a source of embarrassment to a young person. David (Case 4) tells on page 68, and on the companion website, of the time his four-year-old daughter commanded him not to speak English to her in the street, while Loretta (Case 5) as a teenager felt that her mother was too elegant and different. A second language at home can get in the way of more fun activities, as in Case 6, where Adam talks about having to miss football with his friends to work with his Czech, or it can interfere with their command of the majority language, as experienced by Anders and Patrik, who both feel they use more English words and expressions in Swedish than their friends.

The regrets that are expressed here have more to do with missed opportunities or with parents who for one reason or another chose not to speak their language to their children. In some cases, adult children take charge of this themselves, as in the case of Benjamin (Case 9), who goes to Istanbul to learn Turkish, or Loretta's children (Case 5), who are interested in learning Italian, or Pia's children (Case 7), who have a go at speaking Danish to their relatives. They find that even passive knowledge of a language they heard in childhood helps them to learn it when the time comes.

Chapter 11

Research and further reading

Bilingualism and multilingualism are often presented as a problem that has to be addressed or dealt with somehow. But in fact, most of the world's population speak more than one language on a daily basis. There are fewer than 200 countries in the world and an estimated 6,000 languages (Li Wei 2000a: 3), so it is clear that in many countries, knowledge of several languages will be necessary. In the introduction to their *Handbook of Multilingualism and Multilingual Communication*, Auer and Li Wei (2007: 2) ask whether it would not be more logical to view monolingualism as a problem, albeit a curable one. Nonetheless, monolingualism is generally treated as some kind of norm that bilingualism and multilingualism are compared to. Auer and Li Wei explain that part of the reason for this may be that the discipline of linguistics has emerged from European thinking about language, where nation states have been associated with a single language. This is not, of course, to say that European countries have ever been genuinely monolingual, as we saw in the stories from the Iberian Peninsula in Chapter 10.

This chapter is more technical than other sections of the book, and it is intended to give a survey of some of the interesting research that has been carried out into the field of children's bilingual language development. The information given here is by no means complete, but it should serve to give some information to those who want to know a little more, and the references given here will suffice to set those whose interest is deeper on the path to further reading. Once you start reading your way into a field such as childhood bilingualism you find that each paper or book will lead to dozens of others, but that some names, those whose research is particularly central or new, will recur in many reference lists. If you find this kind of research survey uninteresting, you are, naturally, free to skip this chapter!

Advantages and possible disadvantages of bilingualism

One of the questions which have attracted attention both from the research community and from the interested public, including parents considering raising children with more than one language, is whether there are educational advantages or disadvantages associated with bilingualism. Cognitive differences have been the target of investigations from the earliest studies of the 1920s.

A good deal of research has been carried out into examining the brains of bilingual individuals and looking for differences in the brain structure that can be attributed to bilingualism. This has, of course, value to those who want to understand more about the way the brain works, but the main advantage of bilingualism is obviously that the bilingual individual or society has access to more than one language. Communication can take place not only with other bilinguals but also with monolingual speakers of any of the languages spoken. The communicative advantages listed by Li Wei (2000b: 22–23) concern the relationships which can be maintained by bilingual speakers with parents, extended family and community, as well as the possibility of transnational communication and the incidental effect of people with access to more than one language being more sensitive to the needs of the people they are talking to. Li Wei also brings up cultural and potential economic advantages to being bilingual and refers to research showing cognitive advantages.

Nonetheless, there is a persistent feeling in some quarters that there are significant disadvantages associated with bilingualism. Parents in many parts of the world often come across this attitude, particularly from older people, along with the idea that two or more languages might be too much for a child to cope with. Many parents of young speakers of a minority language are given unwanted advice from outsiders about the dangers of bilingualism. Even teachers and medical professionals may have negative attitudes to bilingualism. Some of this is due to outdated or misinformed attitudes to bilingualism and some of it is most likely down to the way bilingual children learn their languages. The normal language mixing that children growing up with two languages pass through at an early age can be taken as evidence by worried monolingual grandparents and others that a bilingual upbringing will result in neither language being learned properly. This kind of thinking has its origin in early research claims which have since been thoroughly discredited. Early research into bilingualism came about in a climate where ethnic and linguistic minorities were very poorly regarded and bilingualism was viewed with suspicion. In many countries in every part of the world, bilingual children have in the past been forbidden to use the language of their choice in school. This has been systematically used as a method of oppressing linguistic minorities in many different contexts. Early work on bilingual development included, for example, IQ tests which claimed to find that rural Welsh–English bilingual children had a lower IQ than monolingual English speakers from the same area (Saer 1923a, 1923b, 1924). Saer's research has been roundly criticised, as there was no real comparability between the groups of children he looked at (Li Wei 2000b: 20–21; Baker 1988: 11–12). A later attempt to replicate his results using his own data found that his conclusions were not supported in the data. More recent research findings (e.g. Golash-Boza 2005) show that bilingualism is associated with higher academic performance, although this particular study did reflect upon the difficult social situation experienced by many immigrant groups in parts of the United States.

Recent research has consistently found advantages associated with bilingual development. This started with work by Peal and Lambert (1962) on bilingual and monolingual children in Montreal, where it was found that the bilingual children did better than the monolingual children in a wide range of tests. Pearson (2008) gives an excellent and accessible overview of research that has been done in this area, including the results that she and colleagues at the University of Miami found in a longitudinal study of bilingual infants' language development, following 25 children from the age of three months. New findings are continuously being added to what is known about cognitive differences associated with bilingualism. Han (2010), for example, found that bilingual Latino kindergarten children showed greater socio-emotional well-being than monolingual white children, regardless of whether their two languages were balanced or the non-English language was dominant. Even children whose English was dominant outperformed the monolingual children. The group who were at risk in terms of self-control and interpersonal skills in Han's study were the non-English monolingual children.

Ellen Bialystok's research (e.g. Bialystok 2001; Bialystok and Craik 2010) is often referred to as showing that bilingualism is linked with enhanced ability for abstract thinking and advanced flexibility. In the 2010 article with Craik it was found that bilinguals perform differently from monolinguals when it comes to certain kinds of non-verbal tasks, such as ignoring irrelevant information in sorting tasks. There is, however, modern research that shows some negative effects of bilingualism, such as bilinguals having lower receptive vocabulary scores even in their dominant language (Bialystok 2001; Bialystok *et al.* 2010) or having greater difficulty naming objects in pictures (Michael and Gollan 2005). It seems, according to Bialystok and Craik (2010), that there is a genuine negative effect on linguistic performance of having two language systems, and that this effect continues throughout the lifespan (Bialystok *et al.* 2008). This difference has been a cause of concern to parents who have an ambition for their children of being perfect speakers of both (or all) their languages, fully comparable with the proficiency they would have in a single language if they had been raised monolingually. Anders's experience, outlined in the interview with him in Chapter 10, supports these findings. Susanne Romaine (1995: 263) criticises what she has elsewhere called this 'container' view of bilingualism (see also Chapter 8, on semilingualism) as failing to appreciate the flexibility of the brain. There is a feeling that the comparison with an ideal monolingual speaker is not relevant.

Li Wei (2000c), in the concluding chapter of *The Bilingualism Reader*, which presents a selection of original papers and excerpts representing seminal research into bilingualism from the 1950s onwards, asks the question what the agenda of the bilingualism researcher actually is. He suggests that the researcher's own mono- or bilingualism, attitude to bilingualism and ethnic origin, as well as age, gender and educational background, will have an effect on what it is that he or she is trying to show in the research undertaken. This in turn will necessarily influence the choice of material and speakers chosen for analysis. Historical events and trends will set the scene for all research, and considerations of language policy and migration policy will always be relevant for the context in which bilingualism research is carried out.

How bilingual acquisition works

Readers wanting to know more about infant bilingual acquisition will find a lot of fascinating material in Yip and Matthews (2007). This text contains many examples from the speech of children growing up with Cantonese and English in Hong Kong, as well as a deeper presentation of the theoretical framework into which much current research into childhood bilingualism fits.

Input

One of the aspects of child language acquisition that has puzzled linguists, even in cases where just one language is involved, is how children manage to learn to speak a language so well when they receive so little input. This is referred to in the literature as the 'poverty of the stimulus' (e.g. Chomsky 1980; Hornstein and Lightfoot 1981). This has been taken as evidence for the innateness of the ability to learn language and what is known as Universal Grammar (Baker and McCarthy 1981). In the case of bilingual acquisition, the problem is compounded by the child needing input in both languages.

One system or two?

On the theoretical level, the organisation of the linguistic systems of the bilingual child's languages has been of interest. Researchers have attempted to find out whether there are two separate language systems developing at the same time from the beginning, or if the languages are initially not separated in this way. Genesee and Meisel, both in 1989, were among the first to ask this question explicitly. Their papers are reproduced in Li Wei (2000a). Meisel found evidence for children consistently using different and appropriate word order for different languages, taking this as evidence for separate systems at work. Genesee pointed out that the way young children mix their languages suggests that they might not actually be able to tell them apart, but goes on to show that there is evidence that infants are, in fact, able to distinguish their languages from the beginning and to use them in 'functionally differentiated ways'. This conclusion has been substantiated by recent research into the amazing linguistic ability of newborn and very young children carried out in Canada (Byers-Heinlein *et al.* 2010), where it is shown that in children who are exposed to two languages throughout gestation the process of bilingual acquisition has already begun by the time the child is born.

Dominance and transfer

Usually, children growing up with two or more languages will have one language which is stronger than the other(s). There are a number of ways this can be seen. A child might have a silent period in one language, where she understands what is said to her in the language but does not speak it. Two of Yip's and Matthews's own children are reported to have gone through silent periods. In some cases this silent period might be very long indeed, and come to characterise the family's communication pattern so that a parent might speak the minority language to the child and be answered in the majority language. Silent periods like this are also found in second language learners (Krashen and Terrell 1983) as a learner accumulates experience of the language before beginning to use it in production. Yip and Matthews (2007: 81) give an example of this from the Hong Kong Bilingual Child Corpus, where one child was found who clearly preferred to speak English even when being addressed in Cantonese. Another way that it may appear that a child has a stronger language is in the length and sophistication of the child's utterances in each language. The same child in Yip's and Matthews's example was found to produce longer utterances in English than in Chinese (based on the mean length of utterance (MLU) in each language).

The way a child mixes the languages and switches between them can also indicate that one language is stronger than the other. Often a bilingual child will keep the structure of one language and sprinkle it with words from the weaker language. Bernardini and Schlyter (2004) express this theory in their 'Ivy Hypothesis', where the idea is that the dominant language is the wall upon which the leaves of the weaker language are supported.

Delay

Harding-Esch and Riley (2003) discuss similarities between the language development of bilingual and monolingual children. While lateness in speaking is one of the things that many parents of children with two languages are worried about, there seems to be little evidence that there is in fact a delay. A study by Doyle et al. (1978) actually showed first words emerging earlier for bilingual children than for monolingual children. Pearson (2008: 245–54) goes through a large number of studies which looked at the commonly used milestone measures of child language development, such as the production of the child's first syllables, first words and first two-word combinations, and found in every case that the difference between monolingual and bilingual groups of children was within the range of variation thought of as normal in monolingual children. This range is very wide, and it seems that individual factors are more important than whether the child is learning one or more than one language.

Research into the ability of very young children to recognise the sounds of their own language carried out by the team led by Janet Werker (see, for example, Byers-Heinlein et al. 2010) at the University of British Columbia in Canada has shown that very young children not only can recognise their own language or languages when they hear them, but can also distinguish between more than one language that they hear in their surroundings. Whereas babies who are exposed to just one language stop hearing differences between sounds that are not important for their language, babies with more than one language hear differences that are important for both their languages. In situations where there is an overlap between the sound systems of two languages a young child hears, she will hold off on settling for a language-specific way of hearing the sounds until later than monolingual children who hear either of the languages. In one sense this can be viewed as a delay, but actually it is a useful strategy for those learning more than one language to maintain flexibility in this way.

This team of researchers has also looked at the way older infants (14–17 months) learn words. They found that children who have more than one language around them keep their options open longer than monolingual children when deciding whether two similar sounds are the same or different. Bilingual children were a few months older before they were able to distinguish between similar words. Again, in one sense this is a delay, but in another it is an adaptation to the bilingual setting.

But this kind of very subtle distinction is not what parents are concerned about when they wonder if their child's bilingual environment is responsible for a language delay. There is some evidence that part of the problem might be that parents and others do not recognise the child's speech as being real language if they are listening in the wrong language. This has been the case for one of my children, whose grandmother looked after him for a day when he was around two and reported that he had been chatting all day but that she had not been able to understand anything because it was English. It was in fact Swedish, but knowing that he might well be speaking English had led her not to listen for Swedish. Pearson mentions an unpublished doctoral thesis at the University of Miami dealing with this topic of intelligibility in bilingual toddlers (Navarro 1998), where it was found that listeners understood less than one-quarter of the speech produced by children of 26 months regardless of whether the children were monolingual or bilingual. The children's speech was intelligible in context, but not out of context. When the listeners could not understand what a child was saying they were equally unsure about whether the child was speaking English or Spanish.

Some research has been done into the rapid spurts of vocabulary acquisition that all children experience. In the 1990s, standardised ways of measuring normal vocabulary learning were developed for many languages (the MacArthur–Bates Communicative Development Inventories – MCDI; Fenson et al. 2007). These tools made it possible to compare the language development of a single child in one or more than one language with an objective standard, in order to see if the development was unusual in any way.

Children do not learn new words at an even rate, though, rather in fits and starts. This is particularly clear in the case of children learning more than one language. Pearson (2008: 254–56) describes a study at the University of Miami where it was found that bilingual children aged from 10 to 30 months experienced lexical spurts, periods of particularly fast vocabulary development, in one language at a time. Another study at the University of Miami (Pearson 2008: 259) showed that bilingual children from 10 to 16 months had slightly smaller receptive vocabularies in either Spanish or English than monolingual English-speaking children, but their total conceptual vocabulary, 'the number of labels they recognise for things in the world', was significantly larger than for the monolingual children.

So it seems that, while there are differences in the timing of various linguistic milestones for bilingual children, it is not really possible to speak of a typical delay in language acquisition. Two languages are not learned in exactly the same way as one, and the child is able to transfer some of what they learn in one language to the other.

How bilingual speakers use their languages

As was mentioned previously (p. 169), children growing up with more than one language may have greater proficiency in one of their languages and they may prefer to speak that language. In bilingual situations, a choice is always available. Children often respond in the majority language to speech in the minority language. This receptive bilingualism, also called passive bilingualism or asymmetrical bilingualism, is very common in families where the minority language does not enjoy high status in the majority culture. Nonetheless, it is also found in other situations, such as Arnberg's work from 1987, where a group of children raised in English- and Swedish-speaking families in Sweden were found to be disinclined to answer their English-speaking parents in that language.

Much research has been carried out on code switching, which is the term given to speech that contains elements of more than one language. In Chapter 4 of this book there is a discussion of language mixing as it occurs in the early speech of children growing up with two or more languages. The kind of code switching generally referred to in the research literature is also found in the speech of adults in bilingual communities; it is usually deliberate and speakers are generally aware of which language they are speaking. Such code switching is one of the benefits of bilingualism. Two bilinguals in conversation can access their entire linguistic repertoire for communication. Sometimes a word or two will be in a different language because it is possible to be more eloquent in that language; sometimes a concept is culturally bound to one or other language; sometimes speakers may switch for effect. Code switching is one of the most noticeable aspects of bilingual language use. Code switching is interesting for a number of reasons. It provides a window into the way bilingual speakers think in their languages, as shown by Poplak (1980) and Clyne (1987). Poplak's and Clyne's studies looked at constraints on code switching, i.e. when and where it occurs or does not occur. Other studies look at the social and communicative contexts in which code switching occurs, such as the work of Blom and Gumperz (1972) and Myers-Scotton (1988) (all four of these studies are reproduced in Li Wei 2000a).

Yip's and Matthews's study of Chinese–English bilingualism in Hong Kong sheds interesting light on this kind of research into code switching. They found that it was very difficult to distinguish between code switching of the kind associated with adult bilinguals and code mixing of the kind associated with very young bilinguals because in fact the input speech heard by the infants was heavily laced with code switching. In many of the families whose situations are described in this book the parents are monolingual speakers of a minority or majority language. In the Hong Kong context, many parents are themselves bilingual speakers and switch at will between the languages, making it impossible to tell the characteristic mixing associated with the bilingual acquisition of two languages from the adult-type code switching the children hear from the adults around them. The acid test would then be to see whether the children as adults are able to keep the languages separate when communicating with non-speakers of Chinese. However, the variety of English spoken by many people in Hong Kong is thoroughly influenced by Chinese, and contains borrowed elements, which would make it almost impossible to distinguish between mixing, switching and normal Hong Kong English.

All in all, the matter of whether and how children are to be given the gift of two languages must be left in the hands of their parents. While bringing up a child with two languages is not difficult, it requires commitment and perseverance on the part of both parents. There is, as can be seen in this book, a good deal you can do to support your child's development in both their languages. The single most important factor in how successful you and they will be in this respect is, however, your and their motivation.

Organising a workshop on raising children with two languages

The workshop has three primary aims. These are to:

- gather those parents, teachers and others in the local community who are concerned with children growing up with two languages in the hope that they will get to know each other for a mutual exchange of experiences and tips
- establish contact with those who represent the local authorities and schools in questions concerning the position of pupils who have home languages and who may require support in the majority language
- develop ideas together to support children's development in both languages and possibly to make the initial contacts necessary to start minority language groups where children can meet others with the same minority language and develop their language (for example toddlers' group, play-group or Saturday school).

The workshop is designed to fit into an evening, with the option of getting together for a follow-up evening if there is enough interest. A possible arrangement is the following:

Have a number of pages prepared with room for eight to ten names on each. The papers should be labelled with a topic, for example:

- How can we optimise our children's linguistic development?
- How can we help our children to appreciate both their cultures?
- How can immigrant parents improve their knowledge of the majority language?
- How can we get the most out of our family's stay in this country?
- How can we support our children's schoolwork in the majority language if we don't speak it well?
- How can we make the most of an intercultural and/or mixed language marriage?

Select topics on whatever suits the participants' interests. As people arrive have them choose which subject they want to discuss and write their name on one of the papers. Anybody wanting to be in the same group as a friend should write their name on the same piece of paper. Give each participant a name tag they can write their name on and pin or stick on their chest. They can also indicate on the name tag whether they are a parent, teacher or whatever.

7:00   People arrive, register (so they can be informed about further meetings and groups which are set up), choose a topic of interest for group discussion, pay the admission fee if there is one, and settle down.

7:15   Introduction and keynote speaker, with questions from the floor. Your speaker should be someone who can speak knowledgeably about bilingualism, intercultural relationships, children's language acquisition and/or second language learning.

8:00   Getting into groups according to the chosen topic. Each group has a leader assigned by the organiser. If possible, refreshments can be served while the participants are getting into their groups, so they can take their cup with them to the group.

8:15   Groups discuss their topics. They can also brainstorm ideas about their topic. Problems associated with the topics are taken up and maybe solutions are offered and experiences shared. The leaders are well prepared with questions but try to keep in the background of the discussion as much as possible. They should make sure everybody gets a say. The leaders take notes and/or make a mind-map of any brainstorming activities. If all or some of the group want to meet again to set up a regular activity, for example a Spanish language play-group, a French-speaking fathers' club or whatever, this can be arranged. A contact person should be nominated, so other participants can get in touch.

9:00   All participants reassemble. Leaders report on each group's discussion, giving information about any follow-up activities the group participants want to plan.

9:30 onwards
        Panel debate with keynote speaker, representative of the establishment and a couple of well-prepared parents. The subject of the debate could be 'Growing up here with two languages'. Let each participant speak uninterrupted for, say, five minutes and then answer each other. Open the discussion to the floor when it seems appropriate. The discussion can then go on until all participants have said what they have on their minds.

End   The organiser might want to round off with a few words, and maybe suggest having another workshop in the future.

The person organising the workshop needs to work out the following details:

- Think of people you would like to speak at the workshop and make arrangements with them. You need a keynote speaker (maybe a researcher or teacher) and someone who can give a completely different kind of perspective for the final debate, maybe a local politician. Decide on your date with your speakers.
- Find a suitable location. While it is very difficult to estimate how many will come, try to find somewhere where everybody can sit together and listen to a speaker, and then break up into groups for discussion and coffee.
- If you have to pay for the use of the room, or for speakers, you will have to charge admission. Make sure you don't leave yourself out of pocket. There may be money available from some authority or other for this kind of activity.
- Recruit and prepare your leaders for the evening. Apart from being generally helpful, collecting admission fees, giving out name tags, serving coffee, etc., they will need to lead the group discussions and be prepared to report on them so all participants are informed about what all groups have discussed.
- Arrange tea or coffee and biscuits or whatever refreshments are appropriate in your country. You'll also need name tags, pens, paper and any kind of speaking aid, such as a computer and/or a projector, for your speakers if these things are not already in the room.

Ways to support a child's development in two languages

Parent and children groups

The aim of this kind of group is to let minority language parents and pre-school children meet other children and parents with the same minority language to sing and play. Most groups meet once a week for about two hours, but other arrangements are possible. If there is a large minority language community, you may be able to meet more often. Not everyone can come every time.

What do you need?

The first priority is to investigate the matter of funding. There may be money and/or other help available from municipal authorities for this kind of group. Maybe you can also get help from the authorities to find somewhere to have the group's meetings. Otherwise, finding a suitable location is the next problem. You will need either to borrow toys that are already there or to buy your own toys and store them in the room you use. Village halls and churches may have their own play-groups or play areas. Perhaps you can use such a room and borrow the toys without having to pay too much (or even for free). You will need access to toilets and changing facilities.

It can sometimes be difficult to get a group of parents and children together. Some tips for getting to know others with the same minority language are given in the section on networking in Chapter 6. A workshop of the kind described in Appendix A can be a good way to meet others in the same situation as you. You might consider advertising your play-group, either in local shops, religious meeting places, childcare centres, clinics, etc., or in a local newspaper.

You may want to have some kind of snack during the group's meeting. Parents can take it in turn to bring something along if that is what works best. You could have a duty roster where parents can sign up for particular weeks. They can then be responsible for arriving early and getting things ready, staying behind to clear up after the meeting is over, as well as providing the snack. If the group is big, maybe two parents will be needed each time. The parent whose turn it is can also lead the group if any leadership seems necessary, although groups often work out a more or less set order of events. Some activities will need preparation.

Younger pre-school children are not always open to too much organising and may prefer just to play with the toys. If the parents get involved with their play they can make sure there is plenty of language happening. Songs, finger play and a simple story are often all the structured activity the under threes can deal with. Arnberg (1987) gives an example of a possible order of events in this kind of play-group, involving planned free play with dolls or cars, active play with singing games, talking about a topic with pictures, snack, song and finger games, drawing or clay and a story, with each activity being allotted 15–20 minutes. Many of the activities might be beyond the youngest children. This is not a problem, since the parents are available to activate them in some other way. Perhaps the younger ones can play some more with the toys while the older children draw.

Things to bear in mind:

- There should probably be at least 10 children in the group, to prevent it petering out too easily when somebody leaves or cannot come several times in a row.
- It is generally not a good idea to have a child come along with a majority language-speaking parent, unless they usually speak the minority language together. To avoid confusing things the group's meetings must be kept free of the majority language.
- The group is for the children's benefit, not primarily a chance for the parents to chat. Left to themselves children of this age are likely either to use the majority language or just to play quietly by themselves. The parents need to play and talk with the children to stimulate their use of the minority language.

Minority language play-school

The difference between the parent and children groups discussed above and this kind of group is that in a play-school setting the parents leave their children with a teacher or leader. Therefore this kind of group is better suited to older pre-school children, around three to six years old. In some countries children start school during this period, in which case another arrangement may be better. But assuming that a group of three- to six-year-olds can be assembled, this can be a beneficial impetus to their use of the minority language. Of course, the success of this kind of arrangement lies almost entirely in the hands of the teacher. She (such teachers are usually women) will need to be very capable and inspire confidence in young children who do not know her and their parents. Many children, especially the younger ones, might refuse to be left. Many teachers are unwilling to have parents around, especially if only some of the children have their parents there. Nonetheless, the children might need a settling-in period with a parent nearby, perhaps waiting in another room. Could the waiting parents arrange some amusement for themselves? What about playing Scrabble or doing crosswords together or having a reading circle to read books in the minority language and then discuss them? Such activities all play their part in keeping the parents' language skills fresh.

Depending on the size and age of the group, the teacher may need a helper. In some groups, parents take it in turns to help the teacher, but this does not always work out too well in our experience, and it might be better to employ an assistant teacher. Such a group is generally more expensive for parents unless local authorities can subsidise it. The teacher and assistant will usually need to be paid, as well as any rental for the use of a room and the cost of toys, equipment and stationery. This kind of play-school often takes place on one afternoon a week, but if the parents' budget can stretch to twice a week it is probably better from the children's point of view.

Checklist for play-school organisers

The person organising needs to take care of the following matters:

- Funding: balance the books! How much does rent, equipment and teachers' pay cost? Look into grants. How much should parents pay?
- Location: where can the play-school be? (See above for suggestions.)
- Recruit a teacher. She needs to be a native speaker of the minority language, but she should be aware of the majority culture that most of the children have lived in all their lives. We once had a newly arrived American teacher in an English play-school in Sweden who tried to talk to the children about *Star Trek*, which had not been shown in their lifetimes on Swedish TV.
- Get together a group of children. There should probably be at least 12 children in the group. Any monolingual minority language

children are a great asset in the group to help prevent the other children slipping into the majority language.

Saturday school

Once children reach school age they do not have much spare time. They may have a series of activities ranging from football to ballet to chess, as well as all the time they spend with friends, playing computer games and maybe even doing homework. An extra morning or afternoon at school might not stand very high on their list of things to do! Nonetheless, if the minority language community is large enough, it might be possible to get together a group of children to study that language. Many countries offer no provision for home language teaching of children who have a minority language at home, leaving it up to the parents whether their children become literate in the home language or not. Parents might find it easier to support their children's literacy in the minority language together with other children.

Ideally, a qualified teacher should be enlisted to help, but if that is not possible perhaps the parents can pool their resources. The parents need to get together and work out what they want from the Saturday school (which can equally well happen on another day), i.e. whether the children are aiming at going back to school in the home country or if it is enough for them to attain reasonable reading fluency to open the world of children's literature in the minority language. Are the children to learn to write and spell in the minority language? There are materials and support available from home-schooling organisations and groups here and there. Otherwise, parents might contact schools and teachers in the home country for advice about materials and methods.

The practicalities of setting up a Saturday school are not any different from those for the other groups. Funding should be looked into, but may not be available. A room needs to be found, though toys are not necessary. If there are only a few children involved they might be able to meet at each other's homes. A teacher must be recruited if the parents are not to do the teaching. Books and writing materials need to be bought.

Children of school age are capable of making their own decisions about many things. Parents may need to put some work into motivating their children to want to go to school in their free time. However much fun you try to make it, reading and writing are very like what the children do all week at school. If they are not motivated, they will not enjoy their Saturday school, and are unlikely to learn very much.

Good luck in anything you organise for your children!

Documenting a child's linguistic development

On the companion website you will find sheets that you can print out to keep track of your child's language development. Have a file or notebook especially for your notes about your child's languages. You can record anything else you notice about your child's linguistic progress. You can use this documentation and the sheets you fill in to see if one language is maybe slipping behind the other. This may be known and expected, but you will have a measure of what is going on and a chance to see if anything the family changes has an effect on the relative strengths of the child's languages.

Vocabulary

There are several ways you could keep track of your child's acquisition of languages. One way is to test vocabulary at different stages. Sheet 1 (available from the book's webpages) can be used to compare the child's vocabulary in both languages. You can start by writing the child's first 50 words in each language, and letting the next test be six months later. For children up to age three or four you can use a picture book of the kind that has pictures of maybe 100 everyday objects without any text. The idea is that each parent (or other person the child speaks each of the two languages with) sits in turn with the child and goes through the book talking about the pictures, seeing which objects the child can name.

For older children you can find a picture book of the kind that has very detailed pictures with lots going on, ideally so that there is no text visible on the page, or cards that show pictures of familiar objects. The level of difficulty can be increased as the child's language develops. Have a range of materials each time, so there are always some words the child knows in both languages. Make the test into a game, and give children only positive feedback, concentrating on what they know rather than what they do not know. Use the test as a chance to teach new vocabulary and talk about new words. If you repeat the test in each language after six months you might see that the child's vocabulary has increased.

Length of utterance

You may also want some way of documenting and comparing the child's progress in learning to put words together in each language. Crystal (1986: 139–41) suggests measuring a child's mean length of utterance (MLU), which is a measure often used in child language research, where concepts such as 'the two-word stage of language development' (when a child typically uses two-word sentences such as 'Mummy come') have been found useful. Sheet 2 (available from the book's webpages) is intended to be used in conjunction with tape recordings of the child's speech in each language, about 15 chatty minutes in each language. On Sheet 2 you can write out 100 consecutive sentences from the child's speech in each language, such as 'Mine!', 'More milk' or 'I don't want to go to school'. If you have difficulty deciding where a particular utterance ends, leave that one out. You can count the total number of words in the 100 sentences then divide by 100, which gives the mean length of utterance. The above utterances have one, two and seven words, respectively. Up to a certain age you can follow your child's mean length of utterance as it increases in each language. The assumption is that longer utterances are a sign of more complex sentence structures, but after a certain level is reached the measure does not reflect language development, since sentences can become more complex without getting longer and vice versa. You can calculate the MLU as follows:

The total number words in 100 utterances divided by 100 gives the mean length of utterance. The number of mixed words multiplied by 100 and divided by the total number of words gives the percentage of mixing.

Language mixing

Interference between your child's languages is interesting to observe, but you may wish to try to minimise it. It is a good idea to see first how much the languages affect each other, and later if anything you are doing is helping to reduce the mixing. You can use Sheet 2 for this test too, but as well as counting words in each utterance, you can count instances where the child uses a word from the 'wrong' language. An utterance like 'More mjölk' instead of 'More milk' or 'Mera mjolk' would, for example, be counted as having 50 per cent mixing whether it was 'supposed' to be English or Swedish. If you count the total number of words in each utterance and the number of words from the other language you can add them up at the end and get an average for the 100 utterances.

Pronunciation

All children have difficulties with the pronunciation of some of the sounds of a language. Some sounds are simply harder to make than others, such as words where two or more consonants come together at the beginning and/or end of the word, for example *blanket, stop, crunched*. Other sounds are difficult in themselves, such as the <th> sounds in *think* or *the*.

Sheet 3 (available from the book's webpages) is meant for you to 'mark' your child's pronunciation. The idea is that you listen for problems in your child's speech. Some of the problems will be of the kind that a monolingual child might have, while others will clearly be like a foreign accent. You can use any of the material you have recorded, but if you want to get children to say a certain sound you can ask them to read a simple sentence with the sound in or show them a picture of an object whose name contains the sound, or you can say sentences to them and have them repeat after you. It can be very difficult to spot children's pronunciation difficulties when you are speaking to them, but if you listen to their speech on a tape you might notice all kinds of things. You may wish to help your children practise special sounds if they have difficulty with them.

Children with two languages may sometimes speak their minority language with an accent like speakers of the majority language have when they speak the minority language. This probably means that the child is using some of the nearest sounds of the majority language instead of minority language sounds and may be following the phonological rules of the majority language in other ways too, so that a Spanish- and French-speaking child in Spain may have difficulty pronouncing a French word which begins with <sp> – for example, *sport* is pronounced *esport*; or a Swedish- and English-speaking child in Sweden may be reluctant to pronounce the final sound in words like *was* as /z/ rather than as /s/.

The point of keeping track is mostly that it is interesting to look back on, but it is also a way to spot any problems and to see how children progress through the sounds and sound combinations of their languages.

In Sheet 3 you can write the word the child is aiming at and describe what the child is doing wrong. Next time round, say after six months, you can try the problem words again. If the child's pronunciation has improved you may discover new problems which were not noticeable before.

Glossary

Code switching changing from one language to another
Dominant language the language in which an individual is most proficient
First language the language or languages an individual acquires as an infant
Foreign language a language learned in a classroom setting – not the majority language
Fossilisation when a second language learner no longer improves his or her imperfect mastery of the language
Interference the effect that one of the languages spoken by an individual has on another
LI first language
L2 second language
Language acquisition gaining proficiency in a language in a setting where the language is spoken naturally
Language learning gaining proficiency in a language in a classroom-like setting
Language mixing using words from more than one language in a single utterance
Language switching see **code switching**
Majority language the language spoken by most of the people in a country or region, often as their only language
Minority language a language spoken by a small group of people (e.g. a family or an immigrant community)
Native speaker an individual who has the language as his or her first (and often only) language
Near-native or native-like speaker an individual who masters a language so well that native speakers cannot detect any foreignness
One language–one location a system of using languages within a family so that each language is associated with a place rather than a

person – the usual arrangement in this system is that the minority language is spoken at home and the majority language is spoken outside the home

One person–one language a system of using languages within a family and elsewhere so that any two people always use the same language when speaking together

Second language a language acquired later than the first language(s) in a setting where the language is spoken naturally

Bibliography

Arnberg, L. (1987) *Raising Children Bilingually: The Pre-school Years*. Clevedon, UK: Multilingual Matters.

Auer, P. and Li Wei (2007) Introduction: multilingualism as a problem? Monolingualism as a problem? In P. Auer and Li Wei (eds), *Handbook of Multilingualism and Multilingual Communication*. Berlin: Mouton de Gruyter.

Baker, C. (1988) *Key Issues in Bilingualism and Bilingual Education*. Clevedon, UK: Multilingual Matters.

——(1995) *A Parents' and Teachers' Guide to Bilingualism*. Clevedon, UK: Multilingual Matters.

——(2006) *Foundations of Bilingual Education and Bilingualism* (4th ed.). Clevedon, UK: Multilingual Matters.

Baker, C. L. and McCarthy, J. (eds) (1981) *The Logical Problem of Language Acquisition*. Cambridge, MA: MIT Press.

Bernardini, P. and Schlyter, S. (2004) Growing syntactic structure and code-mixing in the weaker language: the Ivy Hypothesis. *Bilingualism: Language and Cognition* 7(1): 49–69.

Bialystok, E. (2001) *Bilingualism in Development: Language, Literacy and Cognition*. Cambridge: Cambridge University Press.

Bialystok, E. and Craik, F. I. M. (2010) Cognitive and linguistic processing in the bilingual mind. *Current Directions in Psychological Science* 19(1): 19–23.

Bialystok, E., Craik, F. I. M. and Luk, G. (2008) Cognitive control and lexical access in younger and older bilinguals. *Journal of Experimental Psychology: Learning, Memory, and Cognition* 34: 859–73.

Bialystok, E., Luk, G., Peets, K. F. and Yang, S. (2010) Receptive vocabulary differences in monolingual and bilingual children. *Bilingualism: Language and Cognition* 13(4): 525–31.

Blom, J. P. and Gumperz, J. J. (1972) Social meaning in linguistic structure: code switching in Norway. In J. J. Gumperz and D. Hymes (eds), *Directions in Sociolinguistics*. New York: Holt, Rinehart and Winston.

Byers-Heinlein, K., Burns, T. C. and Werker, J. F. (2010) The roots of bilingualism in newborns. *Psychological Science* 21(3): 343–48.

Chomsky, N. (1980) *Rules and Representations*. New York: Columbia University Press.

Clyne, M. (1987) Constraints on code-switching: how universal are they? *Linguistics* 25: 739–64.

Crystal, D. (1986) *Listen to Your Child*. Harmondsworth: Penguin.

Cunningham, U. (2003) Temporal indicators of language dominance in bilingual children. In Proceedings from Fonetik 2003, *Phonum* 9: 77–80, Umeå University.

Doman, G. and Doman, J. (2005) *How to Teach Your Baby to Read*. Garden City, NY: Square One Publishers.

Dopke, S. (1992) *One Parent, One Language: An Interactional Approach*. Amsterdam: John Benjamins.

Doyle, A. B., Champagne, M. and Segalowitz, N. (1978) Some issues in the assessment of linguistic consequences of early bilingualism. *Working Papers on Bilingualism* 14: 21–31.

Fenson, L., Marchman, V. A., Thal, D. J., Dale, P. S., Reznick, J. S. and Bates, E. (2007) *MacArthur–Bates Communicative Development Inventories (CDIs): User's Guide and Technical Manual* (2nd ed.). Baltimore, MD: Brooks Publishing.

Flege, J. E. (1987) A critical period for learning to pronounce foreign languages. *Applied Linguistics* 8(2): 162–77.

Genesee, F. (1989) Early bilingual language development: one language or two? *Journal of Child Language* 16: 161–79.

Golash-Boza, T. (2005) Assessing the advantages of bilingualism for the children of immigrants. *International Migration Review* 39(3): 721–54.

Han, W. J. (2010) Bilingualism and socioemotional well-being. *Children and Youth Services Review* 32(5): 720–31.

Hansegard, N. E. (1975) Tvåspråkighet eller halvspråkighet? *Invandrare och Minoriteter* 3: 7–13.

Harding-Esch, E. and Riley, P. (2003) *The Bilingual Family* (2nd ed.). Cambridge: Cambridge University Press.

Hornstein, N. and Lightfoot, D. (eds) (1981) *Explanation in Linguistics: The Logical Problem of Language Acquisition*. London: Longman.

Isbell, R., Sobol, J., Lindauer, L. and Lowrance, A. (2004) The effects of story-telling and story reading on the oral language complexity and story comprehension of young children. *Early Childhood Education Journal* 32(3): 157–63.

Kotsinas, U.-B. (1994) The Stockholm dialect and language change. In G. Melchers and N.-L. Johannesson (eds), *Nonstandard Varieties of Language* (Acta Universitatis Stockholmiensis, Stockholm Studies in English 84). Stockholm: Almqvist and Wiksell.

Krashen, S. D. and Terrell, T. D. (1983) *The Natural Approach: Language Acquisition in the Classroom*. Oxford: Pergamon Press.

Lambert, W. E. (1975) Culture and language as factors in learning and education. In A. Wolfgang (ed.), *Education of Immigrant Students*. Toronto: Ontario Institute for Studies in Education.

Lenneberg, E. H. (1967) *The Biological Foundations of Language*. New York: Wiley.

Li Wei (ed.) (2000a) *The Bilingualism Reader*. London: Routledge.

———(2000b) Dimensions of bilingualism. In Li Wei (ed.), *The Bilingualism Reader*. London: Routledge.

———(2000c) Methodological questions in the study of bilingualism. In Li Wei (ed.), *The Bilingualism Reader*. London: Routledge.

Major, R. (1990) L2 acquisition, L1 loss, and the critical period hypothesis. In J. Leather and A. James (eds), *New Sounds 90, Proceedings of the 1990 Amsterdam Symposium on the Acquisition of Second Language Speech*, University of Amsterdam, 9–12 April.

Meisel, J. M. (1989) Early differentiation of languages in bilingual children. In K. Hyltenstam and L. Obler (eds), *Bilingualism Across the Lifespan*. Cambridge: Cambridge University Press.

Michael, E. B. and Gollan, T. H. (2005) Being and becoming bilingual: individual differences and consequences for language production. In J. F. Kroll and A. M. B. de Groot (eds), *Handbook of Bilingualism: Psycholinguistic Approaches*. New York: Oxford University Press.

Myers-Scotton, C. (1988) Code-switching as indexical of social negotiations. In M. Heller (ed.), *Codeswitching*. Berlin: Mouton de Gruyter.

———(2006) *Multiple Voices: An Introduction to Bilingualism*. Oxford: Blackwell.

Navarro, A. (1998) *Phonetic Effects of the Ambient Language in Early Speech: Comparisons of Monolingual and Bilingual Learning Children*. Miami: University of Miami.

Peal, E. and Lambert, W. (1962) The relation of bilingualism to intelligence. *Psychological Monographs* 76 (Whole No. 546): 1–23.

Pearson, B. Z. (2008) *A Step by Step Guide for Parents Raising a Bilingual Child*. New York: Living Language.

Penfield, W. (1965) Conditioning of the uncommitted cortex for language learning. *Brain* 88: 787–98.

Poplak, S. (1980) Sometimes I'll start a sentence in English y termino en español. *Linguistics* 18: 581–618.

Romaine, S. (1995) *Bilingualism* (2nd ed.). Oxford: Blackwell.

Saer, D. J. (1923a) An inquiry into the effect of bilingualism upon the intelligence of young children Part I. *Journal of Experimental Psychology* 6: 232–40.

———(1923b) An inquiry into the effect of bilingualism upon the intelligence of young children Part II. *Journal of Experimental Psychology* 6: 266–74.

———(1924) The effect of bilingualism on intelligence. *British Journal of Psychology* 14: 25–38.

Saunders, G. (1982) *Bilingual Children: Guidance for the Family*. Clevedon, UK: Multilingual Matters.

———(1984) An interview with a Turkish–English bilingual. *Bilingual Family Newsletter* 1(2): 3.

———(1988) *Bilingual Children: From Birth to Teens*. Clevedon, UK: Multilingual Matters.

Scovel, T. (1988) *A Time to Speak: A Psycholinguistic Inquiry into the Critical Period for Human Speech*. New York: Newbury House/Harper and Row.

Skutnabb-Kangas, T. (1981) *Tvåspråkighet*. Lund: Liber Läromedel.

Swain, M. and Lapkin, S. (1982) *Evaluating Bilingual Education: A Canadian Case Study*. Clevedon, UK: Multilingual Matters.

Weizman, Z. and Snow, C. (2001) Lexical input as related to children's vocabulary acquisition: effects of sophisticated exposure and support for meaning. *Developmental Psychology* 37(2): 265–79.

Yip, V. and Matthews, S. (2007) *The Bilingual Child*. Cambridge: Cambridge University Press.

Index

academics, visiting 11
accent: 'artificial' bilingualism 48–49; bilingual case studies 140, 142, 143–44, 145, 158; critical period hypothesis 62–64; culture and 107; immigrants 69, 115; minority language 17–18, 59, 183; minority language and school language 73–74; mixed language families 3, 8; Portuguese-English 112; quality of input 110; regional 143–44; semilingualism 114; Swedish-English 183
active and passive languages 54–57
alphabetic systems 66, 75, 90
Arabic: active and passive languages 57; alphabetic system 66, 90; attitudes to minority language 28; childhood experiences 154, 155; family language system 42
Armenian 14
Arnberg, L. xi, 37, 38, 39, 172, 178
au pairs 19, 48, 80, 116
Auer, P. 165

Baker, C. xi, 167
Baker, C. L. 169
Bernardini, P. 170
Bialystok, E. 167, 168
bilingual: acquisition 168–72; development 40–41; home 12, 78
bilingualism: advantage for adult life 19–20; advantages and possible disadvantages 166–68; 'artificial' 47–50; asymmetrical 172; balanced 17–19; changed circumstances 115–21; how bilingual acquisition works 168–72; how bilingual speakers use their languages 172–73; making plans 20–23; motivation 124–26; names 23–24; passive 172; receptive 172; research 165; views on 41–42
Blom, J. P. 173
brain 62, 166, 168
Byers-Heinlein, K. 169, 170

Cantonese 131, 168, 170
Castilian Spanish 128, 136, 142–44
Catalan 19, 20, 32, 74, 136–38
childhoods, bilingual 164; Catalan-Castilian 136–38; Farsi-Czech-English 147–49; Hindko, Pashto, Punjabi, English Urdu 151–53; Igbo-Nigerian Pidgin English, English, Yoruba 138–40; Italian-English 144–47; Krio, English, Mende 157–60; Latvian-Russian 140–42; Scots-English 142–44; Swedish-Danish 149–51; Swedish-English 160–64; Turkish-Swedish 153–57
children with two languages 66; advantages and disadvantages 65–67; being different 67–71; bringing home friends 69–71; children's culture 103–4; day-care and school 71–77; feeling at home 95–97; grown-up 135; home language

education and Saturday schools
79–82; keeping track of their
development 87–88; knowing how
to behave 97–98; learning to read in
minority language 90–91; linguistic
development 181–84; listening to
86–87; looking back on a bilingual
childhood 135–36; media available
for 91–92; next generation 135–36;
parental role 78; reading to 89–90;
self-image as speakers of minority
language 125; special needs 121–23;
talking to 85–86; teenagers 126–30;
visiting grandparents in another
country 95–97; ways to support a
child's development in two
languages 177–80; working
systematically with 125–26
Chinese: bilingualism study 170, 173;
Cantonese 131, 168, 170; Confucius
Institute 81; culture 102, 106; home
schooling 85; literacy 66, 90;
Mandarin 62; OPOL method 35;
parental input 62
Chomsky, N. 169
Clyne, M. 173
code switching 151, 172–73
Craik, F. I. M. 167, 168
critical period hypothesis 62–64
Crystal, D. 87, 182
cultural competence: achieving 99;
children's culture 103–4; food
and drink 107–8; hospitality 106–7;
men and women 108–9; social
behaviour 100–103; traditions
104–6
cultures, access to two 93–98
Cunningham, U. 23, 39
Cunningham-Andersson, U. 23
Czech 18, 36, 105–6, 147–49, 164

Danish 15–16, 32, 48, 149–51, 164
day-care 71–72
dialect 73, 157, 158
divorce 116–18
Doman, G. 90
Doman, J. 90
Dopke, S. 38, 113, 132
Doyle, A. B. 170
Dutch 34, 44, 64, 97, 105, 117

education: bilingual and minority
language schooling 76–77; day-care
and school 71–72; home language
79–82; home schooling 76, 85, 102,
126, 180; literacy 75–76; minority
language play-school 82, 178–80;
Saturday school 79, 82, 180; school
language 73–75
English: active and passive languages
55, 57; adjusting to setbacks 119–20;
advantage for adult life 19–20;
advantages and disadvantages of two
languages 66–67; advice from other
parents 131–32; 'artificial' bilingualism
47–50; attitudes of strangers 25–26,
28; being able to communicate with
relatives 15, 16; being different 68;
bilingual and minority language
schooling 76–77; bilingual
programme at school 19; bilingualism
studies 167, 168, 170–73; bringing
home friends 70–71; childhood
experiences 138–40, 142–49, 151–53,
155–64; children with special needs
122–23; critical period hypothesis
64; culture 97–98; day-care and
school 71–75; divorce 118; family
language system 31–32; family life
with two languages 22–23, 27; home
language education 79; hospitality
106; intelligibility of toddlers 171;
interference and mixing 58–62;
international language 11, 94–95;
international schools 10; language
attrition 111–13; language choice 2–3;
language development 52–54;
language mixing 5–6, 19; language
and personality 33; language
switching 7; literacy 75–76; minority
communities 14; motivation 124–28;
names 23–24; networking 81;
obtaining material 92; one
language–one location method 45–47;
one person–one language method
36–41, 43–44; parents with two
languages 34; play-school
organisation 179; practical advice
83–84; pronunciation 112, 183;
reading to your child 89–90; school
language 29; social behaviour 100

families: being able to communicate
  with relatives 15–16;
  communication 7–8; developing a
  language system 31–35; minority
  language 8–11, 13–14; mixed
  language 1–8; reactions from the
  folk back home 28–30;
  understanding each other 3–4
Farsi 18, 34, 36, 147–49
Fenson, L. 171
Finnish 14, 47, 49
Flege, J. E. 63
food and drink 107–8
French: active and passive languages
  55; adjusting to setbacks 119;
  advantage for adult life 19, 95;
  'artificial' bilingualism 47–49;
  childhood experiences 148; critical
  period hypothesis 63; day-care and
  school 71; language choice 2, 22,
  27; learning other languages 128,
  138; one language–one location
  method 45; one person–one
  language method 35–36, 40;
  pronunciation 183; school
  language 29

Galician 124–25, 128, 142–44
gender issues 61–62, 108–9
Genesee, F. 169
German: 'artificial' bilingualism 49;
  attitudes of strangers 25; being able
  to communicate with relatives 15;
  childhood experiences 138, 148,
  151, 163; culture 132; feeling at
  home 97; Goethe Institut 81;
  language attrition 113; language
  choice 2; language mixing 6; one
  language–one location method 45;
  one person–one language method
  43–44; practical advice 84–85;
  school language 7, 75, 128; social
  behaviour 100, 102
Golash-Boza, T. 167
Gollan, T. H. 168
grandparents: attitudes to bilingualism
  21, 28–29, 136, 166; being able to
  communicate with relatives 15–16,
  28–29, 67; culture 99;
  grandchildren's visits 95–96, 118,

123; practical advice 83–84;
  religious issues 100; as resources 80;
  traditions 104
Gumperz, J. J. 173

Han, W. J. 167
Hansegard, N. E. 114
Harding-Esch, E. 170
Hebrew 7, 34, 43
Hindko 16, 38, 151–53
home schooling 76, 85, 102, 126,
  180
Hornstein, N. 169
hospitality 106–7

Igbo 38, 138–40
immigrants 9–10; being able to
  communicate with relatives 15–16;
  feeling at home in the immigrant
  parent's home country, 14–15;
  speaking an immigrant parent's
  language 12–13
international employees 10–11
Isbell, R. 89
Italian: being able to communicate
  with relatives 16, 121, 145;
  childhood experiences 144–46, 164;
  culture 69, 121, 145; language and
  personality 33, 69, 145; learning
  another language 137–38; in a
  quadrilingual family 48; Spanish
  and 25

Japanese: culture 97, 102–3; language
  mixing 5; literacy 66, 90; one
  language–one location method 46;
  one person–one language method
  37; out-of-date expressions 111;
  practical advice for parents 84

Korean 34
Kotsinas, U.-B. 115
Krashen, S. D. 169
Krio 157–59
Kurdish 28

Lambert, W. E. 114, 167
language: active and passive languages
  54–57; attrition 110–13; choice 2–3;
  critical period hypothesis 62–64;

developing a language system
31–35; development 51–54;
development delay 170–72;
dominance and transfer 169–70;
how bilingual speakers use their
languages 172–73; input 168–69;
interference and mixing 57–62;
length of utterance 182; losing a
110–12; minority *see* minority
language; mixing 4–6, 57–62,
182–83; one system or two? 169;
parents with two languages 34–35;
and personality 33–34;
pronunciation 183–84; switching
6–7; system 31–35, 39–40, 69, 124,
168, 169; vocabulary 181–82
Lapkin, S. 47
Latvian 19, 140–42
Lenneberg, E. H. 63
Li Wei 165, 166, 167, 168, 169, 173
Lightfoot, D. 169
literacy 75–76

McCarthy, J. 169
Major, R. 63, 112
Mandarin 62
marriage: divorce 116–18;
intercultural 1–8
Matthews, S. 168, 169, 170, 173
Meisel, J. M. 169
men and women 61–62, 108–9
Mende 157–59
Michael, E. B. 168
minority language: bilingual and
minority language schooling 76–77;
communities 13–14; families 8–11;
obtaining material in 91–92;
play-school 178–80; quality of input
110–13; reactions to use of 25–28,
67–69; school language 73–75;
teaching your child to read 90–91;
teenagers' identity 128–30;
teenagers' use of 126–28
motivation 124–26
Myers-Scotton, C. 173

names 23–24
Navarro, A. 171
networking 80–82
Norwegian 25, 72

one language–one location method
44–47
one person–one language (OPOL)
method 35–44

parenting, practical 78
parents: advice from other parents
130–34; death of a parent 118–19;
immigrant 12–15; networking
80–82; parent and children groups
177–78; practical advice for 82–85;
promoting children's self-image 125;
things to do at home 85–92; with
two languages 34–35; using
available resources 79–80; working
systematically with your children
125–26
Pashto 16, 28, 38, 151–53
Peal, E. 167
Pearson, B. Z. 167, 170, 171, 172
Penfield, W. 63
play-school, minority language 82,
178–80
Poplak, S. 173
Portuguese: culture 2; day-care and
school 72; learning another language
85, 128; one person–one language
method 42; pronunciation 112;
responses of strangers 25
pronunciation 60, 63, 112, 183–84, *see
also* accent
Punjabi 16, 38, 151–53

refugees 9–10
relatives: being able to communicate
with 15–16; reactions from the folk
back home 28–30
religion 98–99
Riley, P. 170
Romaine, S. 37, 38, 114, 168
Russian 66, 84–85, 90, 140–41, 163

Saer, D. J. 167
Saturday schools 79, 82, 180
Saunders, G. xi, 38, 49
Schlyter, S. 170
school: bilingual and minority
language schooling 76–77; literacy
75–76; minority language as school
language 73–75; *see also* education